HANDS-ON
FAMILY

KITCHEN SCIENCE LAB

for kids

KITCHEN SCIENCE LAB

for kids

52 FAMILY-FRIENDLY EXPERIMENTS FROM AROUND THE HOUSE

Liz Heinecke

QUARRY

Quarto is the authority on a wide range of topics.

Quarto educates, entertains and enriches the lives of
our readers—enthusiasts and lovers of hands-on living

www.QuartoKnows.com

First published in the United States of America in 2014 by
Quarry Books, a member of
Quarto Publishing Group USA Inc.
100 Cummings CenterSuite
406-LBeverly, MA 01915-6101
www.QuartoKnows.com
Visit our blogs at www.QuartoKnows.com

11

ISBN: 978-1-59253-925-3

Digital edition published in 2014
eISBN: 978-1-62788-040-4

Library of Congress Cataloging-in-Publication Data

Heinecke, Liz Lee, author.
Kitchen science lab for kids : 52 family friendly experiments from around the house / Liz Lee
Heinecke.pages cm
ISBN 978-1-59253-925-3
1. Science--Experiments--Juvenile literature. I. Title.
Q175.2.H45 2014
507.8--dc23
2014004546

Design: Leigh Ring // www.ringartdesign.com
Photography: Amber Procaccini Photography // www.aprocacciniphoto.com

Printed in China

TO CHARLIE, MAY, AND SARAH

CONTENTS

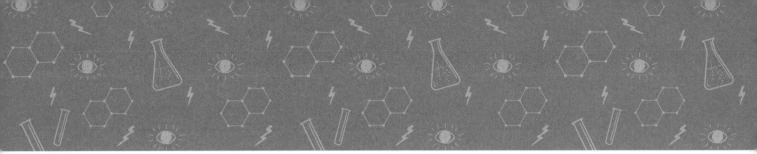

INTRODUCTION

WHEN IT COMES TO INTRODUCING KIDS TO SCIENCE, THERE'S NO PLACE LIKE HOME.

The sparks of curiosity and creativity are first ignited in kitchens and backyards, and these are ideal venues for delving into the amazing world of science. Performing experiments in a familiar environment, without time limits or the pressure of grades, kids discover that science isn't hard or scary, and that they can find it everywhere they look. Best of all, there are a number of projects you can do with what you already have on hand.

When I was young, activities like playing Twenty Questions, collecting rocks, and catching frogs fueled my interest in the natural world, eventually leading me to study science and art. After ten years of bench work in research labs, I embarked on a new adventure: staying at home with three young children.

When my youngest was two, we added Science Wednesdays to the family calendar. Each week, the kids looked forward to trying a science project, taking a nature walk, or visiting a zoo or science museum. It was a fun way to change things up from the usual crayons and play dough.

Unfortunately, many of the experiments I found required specialized equipment, when the last thing I wanted to do was to drag three kids to the hardware store. Calling on my experience in research labs, I started customizing traditional science experiments, and making up a few new ones, with three goals in mind. The projects had to be safe enough for my youngest, engaging enough for my oldest, and would ideally use ingredients I already had around the house.

With our new collection of kitchen pantry experiments, we explored the amazing worlds of physics, chemistry, and biology together. My two-year-old would engage in the projects at the simplest level, often just playing with the ingredients, while my oldest would tackle the science with gusto to see what would happen.

Sunny days found us hunting caterpillars and making s'mores in pizza box solar ovens, while cold and rainy days were livened up by bubbling, color-changing concoctions. We did experiments with yeast and made pizza dough to see how microbiology is used in food preparation. Our backyard became a physics lab for throwing eggs and shooting marshmallows. Litmus paper collages and alum crystal geodes adorned the house as we found beautiful ways to combine science and art.

Our first science journals are now treasured keepsakes, filled with scribbles, illustrations, dates, and awkwardly penned words like "surface tension." The crayon drawings of butterflies, volcanoes, and tie-dye milk are priceless.

To this day, my kids come running when I suggest trying a new or favorite science experiment. I hope yours will too.

OVERVIEW

There's a treasure trove of science experiments hiding in your refrigerator, pantry, and junk drawer. This book will introduce you to 52 fun, educational projects for your family to explore, using things you may already have on hand.

In spring, you might be inspired to study biology by planting a window garden. On snowy winter days, it's fun to try the ice cube experiment to see why plows sprinkle salt on icy roads. Or maybe you have a box of cornstarch on hand and want to keep it simple, by adding water to make a non-Newtonian fluid that's loads of fun to play with.

Each experiment contains an easy-to-understand explanation of the science behind the project to introduce you to the vocabulary and ideas you're exploring. The labs are set up to make science as easy as following a recipe with sections detailing:

→ Materials
→ Safety Tips and Hints
→ Protocol (instructions)
→ The Science Behind the Fun
→ Creative Enrichment

The MATERIALS section lists all the ingredients you'll need to conduct each experiment. SAFETY TIPS AND HINTS will give you some common-sense guidelines for doing the experiments. PROTOCOL is a scientific word for instructions, and each protocol will take you step-by-step through the basics of the experiment. THE SCIENCE BEHIND THE FUN offers simple scientific explanations for each experiment and CREATIVE ENRICHMENT will give you variations or ideas for

taking the project a step or two further. Hopefully, you'll be inspired to come up with some additional ideas of your own.

For kids, science is as much about the process as the results. Measuring, scooping, stirring, and messy hands are all part of the experience, and many of the safe chemical reactions in the book feel cold, are sticky, or have a distinct odor, allowing kids to use all of their senses as they immerse themselves in the experience. Some experiments can even morph into art projects for those who love visual creations. Most are simple to clean up.

Several experiments in this book use the same ingredients. For example, if you're making red cabbage juice for a magic potion, you can use the leftover juice to make litmus paper.

My kids and I have tested all of these experiments, and they will work well if you follow the protocol closely. However, some may involve tweaking or practice for perfect results. Remember, mistakes and troubleshooting are far more educational than perfection, and in science, many laboratory blunders have led to great discoveries.

SCIENCE JOURNAL

Every scientist keeps a notebook to document and detail studies and experiments. The scientific method involves asking a question, making observations, and performing experiments that address the question.

If you want to make your own science journal, find a spiral notebook, composition book, or staple some blank pieces of paper together. Write your name on the cover and use your notebook to keep track of all the great experiments you do. Take your journal on nature walks or vacations and use it to keep track of the plants, animals, and rock formations you spot.

Here's how to keep a notebook like a real scientist, using the scientific method:

1. WHEN DID YOU START THE EXPERIMENT?
Write the date at the top of the page.

2. WHAT DO YOU WANT TO SEE OR LEARN?
Pose a question. For example, "What will happen when I mix baking soda and vinegar together in a bottle?"

3. WHAT DO YOU THINK WILL HAPPEN?
Build a hypothesis. A hypothesis is defined as a tentative explanation for an observation, phenomenon, or scientific problem that can be tested by further investigation. In other words, it's a guess about what might happen based on what you already know.

4. WHAT HAPPENED WHEN YOU DID YOUR EXPERIMENT TO TEST YOUR HYPOTHESIS?
Record your results by measuring, writing, drawing, or photographing the results. Tape photos into your notebook.

5. DID EVERYTHING GO THE WAY YOU THOUGHT IT WOULD?
Look at the information you've collected (your data) and draw a conclusion. Were the results in line with what you thought would happen? Did they support your hypothesis?

After you've done the initial experiment, think of other ways you could address the question, try some of the enrichment activities, or invent a new experiment, based on what you just did. How can what you learned be applied to the world around you? Write down your thoughts in your notebook, in case you want to come back to them some day.

UNIT
01

CARBONATED
CHEMICAL REACTIONS

THERE ARE MANY SIMPLE CHEMICAL REACTIONS YOU CAN DO WITH INGREDIENTS YOU HAVE IN THE KITCHEN. IN FACT, EVERY TIME YOU MAKE COOKIES OR PANCAKES, YOU CREATE A CHEMICAL REACTION TO MAKE THEM RISE.

What's a chemical reaction? It's simpler than you might think.

Everything in our world is made of tiny pieces called atoms. Atoms are often connected to other atoms to form groups of linked atoms called molecules. A water molecule, for example, has two hydrogen atoms and one oxygen atom, bonded together.

A chemical reaction occurs when you mix two different kinds of molecules together to make one or more new kinds of molecules. In other words, it's just mixing two things together to make something new. You can often tell chemical reactions are happening when you see bubbles, feel a temperature difference, notice an odor, or watch a color change.

This unit contains fun chemical reactions that let you mix things together to make carbon dioxide gas.

COLOR-CHANGING MAGIC POTION

MATERIALS

→ Head of red cabbage

→ Knife

→ Pot

→ Blender (optional, see note)

→ Water

→ Heatproof spoon

→ Clear glasses, jars, or small bowls

→ Colander

→ White paper towels

→ 1 heaping teaspoon (5 g) baking soda

→ 3 tablespoons (45 ml) white vinegar

SAFETY
TIPS & HINTS

An adult should boil the cabbage and strain the hot liquid.

This experiment may overflow, so have the paper towels ready.

MAKE RED CABBAGE JUICE CHANGE COLOR AND FOAM OVER IN THIS BRILLIANT, BUBBLY EXPERIMENT.

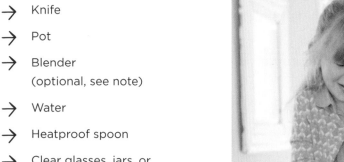

Fig. 5: The bubbles contain carbon dioxide gas.

PROTOCOL

STEP 1: Chop a head of red cabbage into small pieces and place it in a pot with enough water to cover it completely.

STEP 2: Boil the cabbage uncovered for about 15 minutes, stirring occasionally.

STEP 3: Remove from the heat, let the juice cool, and strain the purple juice into a jar or bowl. Pour about ¼ cup (60 ml) of the cabbage juice, or "magic potion," into each of two clear glasses, jars, or bowls and set them on a white paper towel.

STEP 4: Add the baking soda to one glass of cabbage juice and stir. Observe the color change. (Fig. 1)

Fig. 1: Add the baking soda to one glass of cabbage juice.

Fig. 2: Add the vinegar to the other glass of cabbage juice.

Fig. 3: Pour the pink cabbage juice into the blue cabbage juice.

Fig. 4: Watch the chemical reaction.

STEP 5: To the second glass, add the vinegar and see what color it turns. (Fig. 2)

STEP 6: Pour the glass of cabbage juice containing vinegar (pink) into the glass of cabbage juice containing the baking soda (blue/green). (Fig. 3)

Note: To avoid needing to use the stove, chop half of a head of red cabbage and blend it in a blender with about 3 cups (710 ml) of water. Strain the liquid through a colander and then through a coffee filter in a plastic bag with one corner cut off. Blended cabbage juice makes longer-lasting bubbles and turns a slightly brighter shade of blue.

THE SCIENCE
BEHIND THE FUN:

Pigments are molecules that give things color. The pigments in red cabbage juice change shape and absorb light differently depending on whether they're exposed to an acid or base. This makes them change color, so we call them acid-base indicators.

Vinegar is an acid and turns the potion pink. Baking soda is a base, which turns the pigment in cabbage juice blue or green.

When you mix the juice containing vinegar and the juice with baking soda together, a chemical reaction occurs. One product of the reaction is carbon dioxide gas, which makes your solution foam.

CREATIVE
ENRICHMENT

Try adding some other liquids to your magic potion. Can you tell whether they're acids or bases?

Use your cabbage juice to make litmus paper (see Lab 29, "Red Cabbage Litmus Paper") and the leftover cabbage for dinner.

PAPER BAG VOLCANO

MATERIALS

→ Paper lunch sack or small paper bag

→ Scissors·(optional)

→ Tape

→ Empty plastic water or soda bottle

→ White vinegar

→ Food coloring

→ ¼ cup (55 g) baking soda (plus more for step 9)

MAKE A KITCHEN-TABLE KRAKATOA.

PROTOCOL

STEP 1: Invert the brown paper bag and cut or tear a small triangle off one corner to form a hole. This will be the mouth of your volcano.

STEP 2: Tear, cut, fold, crumple, and tape the bag to form a cone shape that will sit over the bottle, with the mouth of the bottle sticking through the cut corner of the bag, but don't tape the bag to the bottle. Decorate your volcano.

STEP 3: Remove the bottle from the bag and fill it halfway full of vinegar. (Fig. 1)

STEP 4: Add several drops of food coloring to your "lava." (Fig. 2)

STEP 5: Place the bag back over the bottle to hide the lava container.

Fig. 1: Add vinegar to the bottle.

STEP 6: Tape a piece of paper together to form a cone with a hole on one end that will fit inside the mouth of your volcano. You'll use this as a funnel to add the baking soda.

STEP 7: Place the volcano in a tray or container to contain the overflow.

Fig. 2: Use food coloring to tint your lava.

STEP 8: Start the eruption by quickly pouring ¼ cup (55 g) of baking soda through the cone into the volcano. Remove the cone immediately. (Fig. 3, 4)

STEP 9: When your volcano stops erupting, try adding more baking soda to see what happens.

Fig. 3: Pour the baking soda into your volcano.

Fig. 4: Stand back!

THE SCIENCE
BEHIND THE FUN:

The volcano you constructed erupts when the baking soda combines with the vinegar to produce bubbles of carbon dioxide gas, which is one of the gases spewed by real volcanoes.

Real volcanoes erupt with much greater force. When Krakatoa erupted in 1883, the explosion and resulting tsunamis killed around forty thousand people, forever changed the geography of the East Indies, spewed tons of sulfur dioxide and ash into the atmosphere, and resulted in some of the most spectacular sunsets in recorded history.

CREATIVE
ENRICHMENT

How much baking soda do you have to add to one cup (235 ml) of vinegar until it stops foaming?

LAB 03

FIZZY BALLOONS

MATERIALS

→ Medium-sized balloon

→ An empty 16 oz soda or water bottle

→ $\frac{1}{3}$ cup (80 ml) vinegar

→ 3 teaspoons (14 g) baking soda

→ Spoon

SAFETY
TIPS & HINTS

It's a good idea to wear safety goggles or sunglasses to protect your eyes, since vinegar is a mild acid and can sting if the balloon accidentally shoots off the bottle.

WATCH A BUBBLY CHEMICAL REACTION INFLATE A BALLOON WITH INVISIBLE CARBON DIOXIDE GAS.

PROTOCOL

STEP 1: Pour $\frac{1}{3}$ cup (80 ml) vinegar into the soda bottle.

STEP 2: Hold the mouth of the balloon open and use a spoon to pour 3 teaspoon (14 g) or so of baking soda into the balloon. This takes two people, one to hold the balloon open and one to add the soda. (Fig. 1)

STEP 3: Shake the soda down into the "bulb" or the main part of the balloon. Carefully stretch the mouth of the balloon completely over the mouth of the bottle, keeping the main part of the balloon off to one side, so the baking soda isn't dumped into the bottle until you're ready. (Fig. 2)

STEP 4: Holding the mouth of the balloon on the bottle, shake the soda into the bottle, all at once. (Fig. 3)

Fig. 1: Add baking soda to the balloon with a helper.

Fig. 2: Put the mouth of the balloon over the bottle's mouth, but keep the baking soda off to one side.

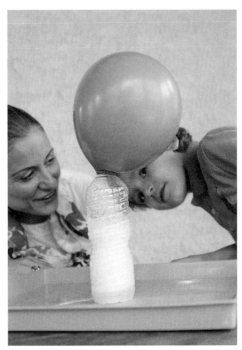

Fig. 3: Shake the baking soda into the bottle quickly, all at once.

THE SCIENCE BEHIND THE FUN:

The scientific name for baking soda is *sodium bicarbonate*. Kitchen vinegar is diluted *acetic acid*. When mixed together, these two chemicals react to form some new chemicals, including carbon dioxide gas, which inflates the balloon. We know a reaction is happening because we can see bubbles forming, the bottle feels cold, and the balloon inflates with the invisible gas.

CREATIVE ENRICHMENT

What happens if you use another method to generate carbon dioxide gas? Many living organisms, including humans, produce carbon dioxide gas when they break down nutrients. Could you do a similar experiment using baker's yeast, sugar, and water to inflate the balloon? Do you think it would take longer?

For tips on growing yeast, see Lab 33, "Yeast Balloons."

FRANKENWORMS

MATERIALS

→ Gummy worms candy

→ Scissors or kitchen shears

→ 3 tablespoons (42 g) baking soda

→ 1 cup (235 ml) warm water

→ Spoon

→ Jar or clear drinking glass

→ White vinegar

→ Fork

BRING GUMMY WORMS TO "LIFE" WITH A SIMPLE CHEMICAL REACTION.

Fig. 5: Watch them wriggle and float.

PROTOCOL

STEP 1: Using scissors or kitchen shears, make super-skinny gummy worms by cutting them into long strips. Cut each worm lengthwise at least four times. The skinnier you make your worms, the better they'll work. (Fig. 1, 2)

STEP 2: Mix the baking soda with the warm water. Stir well. Drop your skinny gummy worms into the baking soda solution. Let them soak for 15 to 20 minutes. (Fig. 3)

STEP 3: While your worms are soaking, fill a clear glass or jar with vinegar.

STEP 4: When the 20 minutes are up, fish the gummy worms out of the baking soda solution with a fork and drop them into the glass of vinegar to bring them to "life." (Fig. 4, 5)

Fig. 1: Cut the gummy worms into very thin strips:

Fig. 2: The thinner they are, the better they'll work.

Fig. 3: Soak your gummy worms in the baking soda solution.

Fig. 4: Drop the baking soda-soaked worms into the vinegar.

THE SCIENCE
BEHIND THE FUN:

The gummy worms float and move as the vinegar (acetic acid) in the cup reacts with the baking soda (sodium bicarbonate) you've soaked them in to form carbon dioxide gas bubbles. The gas bubbles are less dense than the vinegar and will float to the surface, pulling the worms with them. This makes the gummy worms wriggle until the chemical reaction stops.

CREATIVE
ENRICHMENT

Why don't full-size gummy worms work well for this experiment? What else could you bring to "life" with this chemical reaction?

SODA GEYSER

MATERIALS

→ 1 (2 L) bottle Diet Coke

→ Sheet of paper

→ Roll of Mentos mints

CREATE A FOUNTAIN OF FOAM WITH SODA AND MINTS.

SAFETY
TIPS & HINTS

Wear glasses or safety goggles and stand back after adding the mints or you might get soaked. Do this experiment outdoors.

PROTOCOL

STEP 1: Remove the lid from the Diet Coke and set the bottle on a flat surface.

STEP 2: Roll the paper into a tube so it will just fit into the mouth of the bottle. The tube must be big enough to hold the mints. (Fig. 1)

STEP 3: Put your finger over the hole in the bottom of the tube and fill it with the mints. (Fig. 2)

STEP 4: Quickly empty the mints, all at once, from the paper tube into the bottle and stand back! (Fig. 3, 4, 5)

Fig. 1: Make a paper tube for the mints.

Fig. 2: Fill the tube with mints.

Fig. 3: Empty the mints from the tube into the bottle.

Fig. 4: The mints will react with the Diet Coke to make carbon dioxide gas.

Fig. 5: Stand back!

THE SCIENCE
BEHIND THE FUN:

Scientists think the sweetener and other chemicals in the Diet Coke react with chemicals in the Mentos mints. Carbon dioxide bubbles from the reaction form very quickly on all the tiny holes on the rough, pitted surface of the candy. This causes an enormous release of carbon dioxide bubbles that builds pressure in the bottle and sends a jet of soda and bubbles shooting into the air.

CREATIVE
ENRICHMENT

How well does this experiment work with different sodas or mints? Will it work with fruit Mentos?

CRYSTAL CREATIONS

WE LIVE IN A WORLD OF INSTANT GRATIFICATION. GROWING CRYSTALS TEACHES KIDS THAT YOU CAN'T RUSH NATURE. ALTHOUGH CRYSTALS CAN TAKE WEEKS TO GROW, SUCH PROJECTS AS MAKING ROCK CANDY CAN HAVE A GREAT PAYOFF AT THE END.

Crystals are geometric grids of atoms. Imagine a three-dimensional chain-link fence and you'll get the picture. From the salt crystals on your table to the silicon crystals that make up semiconductors, LED displays, and solar cells, we depend on these ordered networks of molecules to enhance our lives.

In this unit, you'll use supersaturated solutions to grow three types of crystals: alum, sugar, and salt. All of the ingredients can be picked up at your local grocery store, if you don't already have them on hand.

ALUM CRYSTAL GEODES

MATERIALS

→ ¾ cup (160 g) alum (potassium aluminum sulfate [see note]), plus more for sprinkling, from the spice section of the grocery store.

→ 3 whole raw eggs

→ Serrated knife

→ Small paintbrush or cotton swab

→ Glue

→ 2 cups (475 ml) water

→ Small pot, to boil the water

→ Food coloring (optional)

CREATE SPARKLING GEODES BY USING ALUM POWDER AND EGGSHELLS.

Fig. 5: Remove you eggshell from the alum solution and c

SAFETY
TIPS & HINTS

An adult should cut the eggshells in half and boil the crystals

Always wash your hands after handling raw eggs.

PROTOCOL

STEP 1: Using a serrated knife, cut the eggs in half lengthwise and rinse them out. Let the eggshells dry.

STEP 2. Apply a thin layer of glue to the inside of an eggshell, using a paintbrush or cotton swab. (Fig. 1) Sprinkle alum powder on the wet glue and let your eggs dry overnight. (Fig. 2)

STEP 3: Dissolve the ¾ cup (160 g) of alum in the water by boiling the mixture in a small pot. This step requires adult supervision. Make sure all the alum dissolves (it may still look a little cloudy) and let the solution cool. This is your supersaturated alum solution.

Fig. 1: Paint the inside of an eggshell with glue.

Fig. 2: Sprinkle alum crystals on the wet glue.

Fig. 3: Add the alum to the water and boil to dissolve.

Fig. 4: Submerge the "seeded" eggshell in the cool alum solution.

STEP 4: When the solution is cool enough to be safely handled, gently immerse your eggshell in the alum solution. For color, you can add a large squirt of food coloring. (Fig. 4)

STEP 5: Let your project sit undisturbed to grow crystals.

STEP 6: After three days, gently remove your object from the alum solution and let it dry. (Fig. 5)

NOTE: Alum can be found in the spice section of a grocery store or supermarket. Usually four or five small jars will do the trick.

THE SCIENCE BEHIND THE FUN:

Alum, also called potassium aluminum sulfate, is found in baking powder and is used in making pickles. Some crystals, such as alum, will form from supersaturated solutions.

A supersaturated solution is one that is forced to hold more atoms in water (or another solute) than it normally would. You can make these solutions at home by heating the solution and then allowing it to cool.

Crystals can form when a supersaturated solution encounters a "seed" atom or molecule, causing the other atoms to come out of the solution and attach to the seed. In this experiment, crystals grow on the seeds of alum you sprinkled into the glue.

CREATIVE ENRICHMENT

Could you do the same experiment with salt or sugar crystals? How do you think the color gets incorporated into the crystal? Do you think the food coloring disrupts the shape? Will larger crystals grow if you let your object sit in the solution longer?

Try coating other objects with glue and growing crystals on them.

ROCK CANDY

MATERIALS

→ 5 cups (1 kg) white granulated sugar (plus more for step 1)

→ 2 cups (470 ml) water

→ Cake-pop sticks or wooden skewers

→ Medium-size pot, to boil the water

→ Glass containers

→ Food coloring

GROW COLORFUL, DELICIOUS SUGAR CRYSTALS ON A STICK.

SAFETY
TIPS & HINTS

This experiment requires adult supervision for boiling and handling the hot sugar syrup. Once it's cooled down, the kids can take over.

PROTOCOL

STEP 1: Dip one end of the cake-pop sticks or wooden skewers in water and then roll them in the sugar. The sugar should cover 2 to 3 inches (5 to 7.5 cm) of the sticks. Let them dry completely. These are the seeds for the sugar crystal growth. (Fig. 1)

STEP 2: Boil the 2 cups of water and the 5 cups sugar in a medium-size pot until the sugar is dissolved as much as possible. It should look like syrup. Once cool, this is your supersaturated sugar solution.

Fig. 1: Roll the ends of the sticks [in] sugar.

Fig. 2: Add food coloring to syrup and stir.

Fig. 3: Remove the candy from the syrup.

STEP 3: Let the syrup sit until it is no longer hot, and pour into glass containers. Add food coloring and stir. (Fig. 2)

STEP 4: When the colored syrup has cooled to room temperature, set the sugary end of the sugar-seeded cake-pop sticks or skewers into the syrup and let them sit for about a week. Gently move the sticks around occasionally, so they don't stick to the crystals in the bottom of the glass. If the glass container gets too full of crystals, pour the syrup into a new container and move your stick into the clear syrup to grow more crystals.

STEP 5: When the rock candy is done, drain the excess syrup and let the sticks dry. Look at them under a magnifying glass for a close-up look. (Fig. 3)

STEP 6: Bon appétit!

THE SCIENCE BEHIND THE FUN:

Like bricks in a wall, crystals are solids formed by a network of repeating patterns of molecules. Instead of the mortar that holds brick together, the atoms and molecules are connected by atomic bonds.

Crystals that share the same chemical composition can be big or small, but the molecules always come together to form the same shape. Table sugar, or sucrose, is made up of a molecule comprised of two sugars, glucose and fructose. Crystals formed by sucrose are hexagonal (six-sided) prisms, slanted at the ends.

The crystals that make up your rock candy grow larger when the sugar molecules in the syrup bind to the seed crystals of sugar that you rolled onto the stick.

CREATIVE ENRICHMENT

What other surfaces could you grow sugar crystals on? How big will they get? If you leave your rock candy in sugar solution for months, will the crystals continue to grow?

CLIMBING SALT CRYSTALS

MATERIALS

WATCH COLORFUL SALT WATER CLIMB A STRING AND COVER IT WITH TINY CRYSTALS AS IT EVAPORATES.

→ String (white cotton kitchen twine works best)

→ Scissors

→ 4 small, clear containers, such as jars or cups

→ 2 cups (470 ml) water

→ Small pot

→ 8 tablespoons (144 g) salt

→ Food coloring

→ 8 paper clips

→ Magnifying glass

Fig. 5: Check your crystals every day to see how they're growing.

SAFETY
TIPS & HINTS

An adult should boil the water and supervise kids adding salt to hot water.

PROTOCOL

STEP 1: Cut a piece of string about 6 inches (15 cm) long for each container.

STEP 2: Bring the water to a boil in a small pot.

STEP 3: Add the salt to the water, a tablespoon (18 g) at a time, stirring until no more salt will dissolve. When it cools, this is your supersaturated salt solution. (Fig. 1)

STEP 4: Let the mixture cool and then pour about ¼ cup (60 ml) of the salt solution into each container.

Fig. 1: Dissolve the salt in hot water.

Fig. 2: Add food coloring to each jar.

Fig. 3: Tie a paper clips onto the end of each string.

Fig. 4: Submerge the knotted end of a string in each jar.

STEP 5: Add a few drops of food coloring to each jar or cup. Stir. (Fig. 2)

STEP 6: Knot one end of each string you cut and tie a paper clip to the other end. Place the knotted end of a string into each of the containers of colored salt solution. The string will float, so swish it around so it soaks up some salt water. Leave the paper clip end of the string hanging over the outer edge of the container. (Fig. 3, 4)

STEP 7: Check the string every day to see what happens. Observe the crystals under a magnifying glass. (Fig. 5)

THE SCIENCE
BEHIND THE FUN:

The scientific name for salt is sodium chloride, or NaCl. When you add salt to boiling water, you create a supersaturated solution that holds more sodium chloride atoms than it would at room temperature.

In this experiment, the salt water is absorbed by the string and climbs all the way out of the jar. When the water evaporates, the salt absorbed by the string remains in the fibers and bonds to other salt molecules to form new, larger sodium chloride crystals on the string.

CREATIVE
ENRICHMENT

What happens if you mix salt and sugar together in your supersaturated solution? Will all the crystals look the same under the magnifying glass?

UNIT
03

PHYSICS IN MOTION

MANY YEARS AGO IN ENGLAND, THERE WAS A STUDENT WHO LOVED MATH AND SCIENCE. HE STUDIED THE WORK OF GREAT THINKERS, SUCH AS COPERNICUS, GALILEO, AND KEPLER, AND OBSERVED THE WORLD AROUND HIM WITH CURIOSITY AND WONDER.

Legend has it that he saw an apple fall from a tree and came up with the idea of gravity, which gave him a new way to think about the motion of planets. This scholar, whose name was Sir Isaac Newton, published a book in 1687 about motion and gravitation that changed the way people saw the world, the universe, and science in general.

In physics, the motion of an object is defined as a change in location or position with respect to time. A change in motion is the result of some force applied to that object. In this unit, you'll play with motion, force, and energy to see how the force applied to everything from marshmallows to raw egg affects everyday objects. You may even notice the name Newton in a few of the experiments.

MARSHMALLOW SLINGSHOTS

MATERIALS

→ Rubber bands

→ Plastic or rubber ring (such as the kind you find on the neck of a prescription bottle or under the lid of a plastic milk jug)

→ Marshmallows

→ Chair with legs

TRANSFORM ENERGY TO MAKE FOOD FLY.

Fig. 5 It may take a little practice

PROTOCOL

STEP 1: Attach two or more rubber bands to the ring (you can double it to make it stronger) with the ring in the center. You can link two rubber bands by overlapping them slightly, and pulling the bottom one through the one on top and then through itself. Attach them to the ring the same way. (Fig. 1, 2)

STEP 2: Set up your slingshot on a chair by turning the chair over and stretching the rubber bands between the legs, with the ring in the center. (Fig. 3)

STEP 3: Use your slingshot to shoot marshmallows at a target and watch as the elastic energy in the rubber bands turns into kinetic energy, which is the energy of motion. It may take some practice, but before you know it, you'll be a confectionery sharpshooter. (Fig. 4)

Fig. 1: Put a rubber band through a ring.

Fig. 2: Pull one end of the rubber band through the other to make a slingshot.

Fig. 3: Attach your slingshot to the legs of an upside-down chair.

Fig. 4: Shoot marshmallows at a target.

THE SCIENCE
BEHIND THE FUN:

Energy changes, but it doesn't go away, it transforms. This scientific concept is called the transformation of energy. When you pull the rubber band on your slingshot back, your muscles do work on the rubber band. How much work you do depends on how hard you pull on the rubber band (force) and on how far back (the distance) you pull the rubber band. Work = force × distance.

The work you do is stored as elastic energy in the rubber band. When you release the rubber band, the rubber band does work on the marshmallow and the elastic energy is transformed into kinetic energy (the energy of motion) in the flying marshmallow. When the marshmallow hits something and stops, the kinetic energy is transformed into heat energy.

CREATIVE ENRICHMENT

Does the thickness of your rubber bands affect how far you can shoot an object? Why?

What other variables affect the distance and direction of your marshmallow's flight?

TABLECLOTH TRICK

MATERIALS

→ Table

→ Sturdy, heavy bowl or drinking glass that isn't too tall or tippy

→ Seamless tablecloth, easel paper, or old bedsheet with the seams cut off

→ Water

SAFETY
TIPS & HINTS

This is a fun experiment to do outside, since it can take a little practice. Having grass or a soft blanket under the table helps prevent dishes from breaking.

AMAZE YOUR FRIENDS AND FAMILY WITH THIS FEAT OF PHYSICS.

Fig. 3: Ta da

PROTOCOL

STEP 1: Put the tablecloth on the table so it covers about 2 feet (61 cm) of the flat surface.

STEP 2: Fill the bowl or glass halfway full with water and place it on the tablecloth near the edge of the table.

STEP 3: Grasping the tablecloth with two hands, pull it straight down, along the edge of the table, very fast. This is important. If you pull it out, toward you, or pull it too slowly, it won't work. If you do it correctly, the water will slosh a little, but the bowl or glass will remain on the table, full of water. (Fig. 1, 2, 3)

g. 1: Pull the tablecloth upward to prepare.

Fig. 2: Pull straight down, very fast.

THE SCIENCE
BEHIND THE FUN:

The law of inertia says that objects don't want to change the speed at which they're moving (or not moving, in the case of our water glass). The heavier something is, the more inertia it has.

In this experiment, the heavy glass of water is standing still and doesn't want to move. Since the tablecloth is moving under the glass very quickly, the heavy glass slips on it, but doesn't move very far. Even the friction between the glass and the tablecloth isn't a strong enough force to make it move. It might seem like magic, but it's physics.

CREATIVE
ENRICHMENT

What happens if you do this with a heavy plate and silverware? What material works best for the tablecloth? What doesn't work?

EGG-THROWING EXPERIMENT

MATERIALS

→ An old sheet

→ Clothespins, twisty-ties, or string

→ Raw eggs

→ Tree, clothesline, or 2 people to hold the sheet

→ 2 chairs

NEXT TO THE KITCHEN TABLE, THE BACKYARD IS OUR FAVORITE SCIENCE LABORATORY. LEARN ABOUT MOTION AND FORCE BY THROWING EGGS.

PROTOCOL

STEP 1: Hang the sheet from a tree by attaching it to branches using clothespins, twisty-ties, or string. If you don't have a tree, hang the sheet from something else, or have two assistants hold it up.

STEP 2: Have two people hold the bottom of the sheet up to form a J shape, or tie it to two chairs. (Fig. 1)

STEP 3: Throw a raw egg at the sheet as hard as you can. It won't break because the sheet slows the movement of the egg as it comes to a stop. (Fig. 2)

Fig. 1: (above) Have two people hold the bottom of the sheet up to form a J shape.

Fig. 2: (left) Throw the eggs at the middle of the sheet as hard as you can.

Fig. 3: The eggs will not break.

What happens if you change the speed of the egg quickly, with lots of force? Tape newspaper to the side of your garage or to a table turned on its side. Throw an egg at the hard surface. Don't forget to clean up! A garden hose should do the trick.

THE SCIENCE BEHIND THE FUN:

An object in motion wants to remain in motion. To stop an egg that's moving through the air, you have to apply force to the egg. In this experiment, the force is applied by a hanging sheet.

The law of motion says that the faster you change the speed of an object, the greater the force applied to the object will be. When you change the speed of the egg slowly, like the sheet does, it lessens the force applied to the egg and the egg remains intact.

This is why they put airbags in cars. If a car is moving and hits something, causing it to stop very quickly, the airbag acts like the sheet, slowing the person in the car down SLOWLY and greatly reducing the amount of force with which they hit the dashboard.

EGG IN A BOTTLE

MATERIALS

→ A glass bottle, such as a juice bottle, whose neck is a little smaller than a hard-boiled egg

→ Small or medium-size hard-boiled eggs

→ Banana

→ Knife

→ Birthday candles

→ A long match or lighter

SAFETY
TIPS & HINTS

This experiment requires adult supervision, since it requires the use of a match or lighter. The upside-down protocol is a little easier.

WATCH ATMOSPHERIC PRESSURE PUSH AN EGG INTO A BOTTLE, AS IF BY MAGIC.

Fig. 1   Fig. 2

FLIPPED PROTOCOL

STEP 1: Put two birthday candles in the wide end of a hard-boiled egg.

STEP 2: Light the candles and hold them under the inverted bottle to warm the air inside.

STEP 3: Hold your bottle upside down and put the candle end of the egg up into the bottle so it forms a seal. Continue to hold the egg until the candle goes out and the egg is "pushed" into the bottle by atmospheric pressure, which is the weight of the air pushing on the egg. (Fig. 1, 2)

STANDARD PROTOCOL

STEP 1: Peel a hard-boiled egg, set it on the mouth of the glass bottle, and verify that it won't easily squeeze through. Remove the egg. (Fig. 3)

STEP 2: Cut a thick slice of banana as your "candle holder," stick a candle into the banana slice, and drop it into the bottle so the candle is pointing up.

STEP 3: Light the candle and set the egg on the bottle so that it forms a tight seal. Wait for the candle to go out and see what happens. If it doesn't work, try the flipped bottle protocol. (Fig. 4, 5)

Fig.3: Peel an egg.

THE SCIENCE
BEHIND THE FUN:

The flame from the candle heats the air in the bottle. When the candle goes out from lack of oxygen, the remaining air in the bottle cools rapidly, decreasing the air pressure in the bottle and creating a partial vacuum. The outside air, whose atmospheric pressure is higher, pushes the egg into the bottle as it attempts to equalize the pressure inside of the bottle.

Fig. 4: Light the candle and set the egg on the mouth of the bottle.

Fig. 5: Watch atmospheric pressure push the egg into the bottle.

UNIT
04

LIFE SCIENCE

LIVING THINGS ARE MARVELOUS MOSAICS OF MOLECULES.
RESEARCHERS WHO STUDY THE COMPLEXITIES OF LIVING
SYSTEMS HOPE TO MAKE DISCOVERIES THAT WILL MAKE THE
WORLD A HAPPIER, HEALTHIER PLACE FOR ALL LIVING CREATURES,
INCLUDING US.

From chicken eggs to DNA, it's fun to explore the science of life at home. This unit investigates eggshells, demonstrating how the amazing architecture of life can be strong and fragile at the same time. You'll also learn how to extract DNA from strawberries and how to lift fingerprints using scotch tape. While our DNA makes each of us unique at a molecular level, our fingerprints are physical manifestations of our individuality.

ALIEN MONSTER EGGS

MATERIALS

→ Jar large enough to hold your eggs

→ Whole raw eggs (in the shell)

→ Permanent markers (optional)

→ White or cider vinegar

→ Green food coloring

→ Corn syrup

SAFETY
TIPS & HINTS

Remember to always wash your hands after handling raw eggs because some carry bacteria that can make you sick!

Be careful not to get vinegar in your eyes since vinegar is a mild acid and stings!

DISSOLVE EGGSHELLS WITH VINEGAR AND USE CORN SYRUP TO SHRIVEL YOUR MONSTROUS CREATIONS.

PROTOCOL

STEP 1: Put some whole raw eggs into a jar and cover them with vinegar. It's fun to use permanent markers to make the eggs look like eyeballs before you put them in the vinegar. (Fig. 1)

STEP 2: Let the eggs sit overnight in the refrigerator. Gently rinse them with water. Only the membrane of the egg will remain, which is like a rubbery balloon. How does it feel? (Fig. 2)

STEP 3: To make alien monster eggs, dump out the vinegar, rinse the eggs, and return them to the jar. Cover them with corn syrup and add some green food coloring. Gently invert the jar to mix. Leave them for 24 hours in the refrigerator. How do they look? (Fig. 3, 4)

Fig. 1: Put whole raw eggs into a jar and cover with vinegar.

Fig. 2: Remove the eggs from the vinegar the next day and observe them.

Fig. 3: Rinse the eggs and add corn syrup.

Fig. 4: Corn syrup will shrivel the eggs.

THE SCIENCE
BEHIND THE FUN:

Eggshells are made up of two chemical elements called calcium and carbon, which are bound together in calcium carbonate crystals. Vinegar is an acid that breaks the crystals apart in a chemical reaction. The calcium carbonate and vinegar react to form carbon dioxide bubbles, which you see when you add vinegar to the eggs.

The balloonlike membrane of eggs allows water molecules to pass through. Corn syrup is mostly sugar and doesn't have much water in it, so water molecules move out of the egg into the corn syrup, causing the egg to shrivel.

CREATIVE
ENRICHMENT

Rinse the eggs and submerge them in water again overnight (in the fridge). What happens?

STANDING ON EGGS

MATERIALS

→ 1 or 2 cartons of 12 raw eggs

TEST THE STRENGTH OF EGGSHELLS BY STANDING ON THEM.

Fig. 4: Distribute your weight evenly and let go

PROTOCOL

STEP 1: Open a carton or two of raw eggs. (Fig. 1)

STEP 2: Make sure that none of your eggs is cracked and turn them so that they're all pointing in the same direction (pointy side up or round side up).

STEP 3: Set the carton(s) of eggs on the floor or driveway.

STEP 4: Remove your shoes and socks and hold onto a chair or someone's hand. Keeping your feet flat, carefully step onto the eggs with your entire foot. (Fig. 2, 3, 4)

g. 1: Eggs are stronger than you think.

Fig. 2: Hold onto someone's hand and step carefully onto the eggs.

Fig. 3: The eggs probably won't break.

THE SCIENCE
BEHIND THE FUN:

Humans use arches to build strong buildings and bridges. Chicken eggs have delicate shells that chicks can peck their way out of, but their arched architecture is nothing short of amazing and allows them to handle large amounts of pressure without cracking. This is extremely important, because their mothers must sit on them to hatch them out.

Pressure is defined as force per unit of area. When you stand barefoot on a carton of eggs, you can equally distribute your weight, and therefore the pressure, among all twelve eggs. Their arched structure is strong enough to keep them from breaking.

CREATIVE
ENRICHMENT

Try the same experiment while wearing a spiked heel, soccer cleats, or track spikes. What happens?

Remove any rings you have on, place a whole raw egg in a resealable plastic bag and wrap your hand around it evenly. Squeeze as hard as you can. Can you break it?

DNA EXTRACTION

MATERIALS

→ 3 strawberries

→ Butter knife

→ A few 1- or 2-cup (235 or 475 ml) liquid measuring cups

→ Fork

→ Measuring spoons

→ Liquid or powdered laundry detergent

→ ½ cup (120 ml) warm tap water

→ 2 medium-large bowls

→ 1 to 2 cups (235–475 ml) very hot tap water

→ 1 to 2 cups (235–475 ml) water

→ Ice cubes

→ Resealable plastic bag

→ Scissors

→ Cone-shaped coffee filter

→ Small, narrow clear vase, cordial glass, drinking cup, or test tube

→ ¼ teaspoon (1.5 g) salt

→ Ice-cold grain alcohol or rubbing alcohol

→ Toothpick, stirring stick, or plastic fork

ISOLATE THE GENETIC MATERIAL DNA FROM STRAWBERRIES.

Fig. 5: Strawberry DNA.

PROTOCOL

STEP 1: Cut the strawberries into small pieces. (Fig. 1) Put the strawberry pieces in one of the liquid measuring cups and mash them with a fork.

STEP 2: Add 1 teaspoon (6 ml or 5 g) of liquid or solid detergent to the warm tap water, then mix and pour this soapy mixture over the strawberries.

STEP 3: Add the very hot tap water to one of the bowls and set the cup containing the strawberries and detergent inside the bowl of hot water. The hot water should not spill into your strawberry mixture. (Fig. 2)

STEP 4: Stir the strawberry mixture again. The detergent and warm temperature will break up the strawberry cells. Proteins called enzymes will start chewing up cell parts, releasing the DNA from the nucleus. Wait 12 minutes, stirring the strawberry mixture occasionally.

STEP 5: When the 12 minutes are up, add 1 to 2 cups (235 to 475 ml) of water and lots of ice cubes to your other large bowl to make an ice bath. Set the cup containing the strawberry mixture into the ice bath to chill for 5 minutes, stirring once or twice. (Fig. 3)

Fig. 1: Cut up some strawberries.

Fig. 2: Put the strawberry mixture into a hot water bath.

Fig. 3: Put the strawberries over an ice bath for 5 minutes.

Fig. 4: Using a filter, strain out the strawberry chunks and keep the supernatant.

STEP 6: While you wait, cut a resealable plastic bag into a funnel the same size as your coffee filter and clip off the corner so liquid can flow out. Put the coffee filter inside your plastic bag funnel. Set the bag containing the filter in your other measuring cup, or a wide glass.

STEP 7: When 5 minutes are up, pour the strawberry solution into the filter/funnel and hold it while the strawberry gunk is filtered out and the supernatant containing the DNA flows through and into the cup below. If your filter gets clogged, use a spoon to carefully remove some of the strawberry gunk. (Fig. 4)

STEP 8: To precipitate the DNA, pour some supernatant into your small, narrow glass until it is about one-third full. Add the salt to the supernatant and mix it well. Gently pour an equal volume (the same amount as your supernatant) of ice-cold alcohol into your supernatent. Put your hand over the top of the glass and rock it gently. Set it down on the table or on ice and let it sit for a few minutes.

STEP 9: You should see a cloudy goo layer form near the top of the liquid. It may look bubbly or slightly white. This is strawberry DNA. Remove some DNA with a toothpick, stirring stick, or plastic fork. It will look like clear slime. Congratulations! You've isolated DNA. (Fig. 5)

THE SCIENCE
BEHIND THE FUN:

DNA, or deoxyribonucleic acid, is a chain of molecules containing genetic information and is sometimes called the "blueprint of life." In such organisms as plants and animals, DNA is stored in a special compartment called a nucleus, where the long, stringlike DNA is tightly coiled. To separate DNA from the organism that contains it, you have to break the cells apart (lysis), filter out the big pieces of cell parts, collect the remaining liquid, or supernatant, and add chemicals, such as salt and alcohol, to precipitate the DNA.

CREATIVE
ENRICHMENT

Try isolating DNA from other fruits and vegetables. What happens if you let some of the strawberry mixture sit in detergent overnight? Can you still isolate DNA?

FORENSIC FINGERPRINTS

MATERIALS

→ 2 sheets of white paper

→ Transparent tape, such as Scotch Tape

→ Pencil

→ Magnifying glass

→ Clear glass or jar

→ Unsweetened cocoa powder

→ A paintbrush or makeup brush

SAFETY
TIPS & HINTS

Be very gentle when dusting prints so you don't smear the image.

DUST FOR FINGERPRINTS AND TRY YOUR HAND AT DERMATOGLYPHICS.

PROTOCOL

STEP 1: On one sheet of paper, trace your left hand with a pencil. If you're left-handed, trace your right hand. (Fig. 1)

STEP 2: On the other piece of paper, scribble hard with the pencil until a small area is covered with the graphite from the pencil lead. Rub your pinkie around in the graphite until it is covered with gray. Carefully place your graphite-covered pinkie finger on the sticky side of a piece of transparent tape and gently lift your finger off the tape. A clear fingerprint should be visible. (Fig. 2)

STEP 3: Place the tape facedown on the pinkie finger of the hand you traced.

Fig. 1: Trace your hand with a pencil.

Fig. 2: Transfer your graphite fingerprint to clear tape.

Fig. 3: Tape your fingerprints to the matching fingers on your traced hand.

Fig. 4: Inspect your fingerprints.

STEP 4: Repeat with each finger of your left hand until you have fingerprints on each of the five fingers you traced. (Fig. 3)

STEP 5: Inspect the fingerprints under a magnifying glass, or with your naked eye. (Fig. 4)

STEP 6:. Rub your hands together to spread the oil on your skin around, then make several fingerprints on a clear glass.

STEP 7: Using a brush, gently dust some cocoa powder onto one of the fingerprints on the glass.

STEP 8: Blow the excess cocoa powder away and lift the fingerprint with a piece of tape.

STEP 9: Tape the fingerprint onto a piece of white paper and try to match it to one from your hand. Can you figure out which finger it came from?

THE SCIENCE
BEHIND THE FUN:

Skin's outer layer is called the epidermis, and a fingerprint is the impression left by epidermal ridges on human fingers. These ridges help us feel things and grip things better. No two people have identical fingerprints, although fingerprint patterns tend to run in families. These patterns tend to look like whorls, loops, or arches, and fingers often leave imprints of sweat, oil, ink, or other substances behind. Fingerprints are often essential tools in crime scene investigations and the scientific study of fingerprints is called dermatoglyphics.

CREATIVE
ENRICHMENT

Make a fingerprint profile for your family members and dust the water glasses from your table after dinner. Can you identify who used each glass?

Try dusting your fingertips with cornstarch, lifting the prints with tape and taping them onto black paper. How do they compare to the ones you lifted using graphite?

ASTONISHING LIQUIDS

WHEN YOU THINK ABOUT EARTH'S IMMENSE OCEANS AND PLENTIFUL LAKES AND RIVERS, IT MIGHT SEEM AS IF THERE'S LIQUID EVERYWHERE. IF YOU'RE FORTUNATE ENOUGH TO LIVE IN A PLACE WITH GOOD SANITATION SYSTEMS, YOU CAN JUST TURN A HANDLE AND CLEAN WATER WILL POUR FROM A FAUCET.

However, because such liquids as water can only exist within a narrow range of temperatures and pressures, they're something of a rarity in the universe. In fact, most of the universe is made up of gases and plasma, with only traces of solid matter and little or no liquid.

Liquids are a type of fluid, meaning they can flow to take the shape of any container you pour them into. They exist somewhere in between solid and gaseous states and can contain multiple types of molecules. The atoms in liquids stick together due to special intermolecular glue known as cohesive forces. The interplay between forces acting on liquids are responsible for many of their interesting behaviors. In this unit, we'll play with some of the unusual properties of liquids.

TIE-DYE MILK

MATERIALS

→ Shallow dish or plate

→ Small cup or bowl

→ Milk

→ Dishwashing liquid or liquid hand soap

→ Cotton swabs

→ Liquid food coloring

YOU'LL BE AMAZED AS YOU WATCH THE FORCES OF SURFACE TENSION AT WORK IN THIS COLORFUL EXPERIMENT.

Fig. 4: Touch the milk with your swab repeatedly to make more colorful patterns.

PROTOCOL

STEP 1: Add enough milk to cover the bottom of the dish. The experiment works best with a thin layer of milk. (Fig. 1)

STEP 2: In the small cup or bowl, mix together 1 tablespoon (15 ml) of water and 1 teaspoon (5 ml) of liquid dish detergent or liquid hand soap. Some detergents may work better than others.

Fig. 1: Add milk to the dish.

Fig. 2: Add drops of food coloring to the milk.

Fig. 3: Touch the milk with your soap-soaked swab.

STEP 3: Put several drops of food coloring into the milk. Space them out in the milk so you can see what happens when you break the surface tension. (Fig. 2)

STEP 4: Dip a cotton swab into the dish soap mixture and then touch the wet swab to the milk. Don't stir! The detergent will break the surface tension of the milk and the food coloring will swirl around as if by magic. (Fig. 3)

STEP 5: You can keep re-wetting your cotton swab with soapy water and touching it to the milk. Sometimes it works to touch the swab to the bottom of the plate and hold it there for a few seconds. (Fig. 4)

CREATIVE ENRICHMENT

How does the fat content of the milk affect surface tension? Does whole milk work better than skim ?

What happens if you vary the depth of the milk in the dish?

Does the concentration of the soap matter? What happens if you put a drop of undiluted dish detergent in your milk?

THE SCIENCE
BEHIND THE FUN:

Imagine that the surface of liquids is a stretched elastic skin, like the surface of a balloon full of air. The scientific name for the way the "skin" of a liquid holds together is surface tension.

When the skin of the liquid is broken by detergent, food coloring and milk move and swirl around in interesting patterns on the milk's surface.

ZOOMING FISH

MATERIALS

→ Large rectangular pan or cookie sheet with sides

→ Heavy construction paper, card stock, thin cardboard, or craft foam

→ Scissors

→ Liquid dish detergent

MAKE A PAPER FISH "SWIM" WITH A DROP OF SOAP AND THE FORCES OF SURFACE TENSION.

Fig. 5: Place a drop of dish detergent in your fish's tail slot.

PROTOCOL

STEP 1: Draw some small fish, around 2 inches (5 cm) long, on paper, cardboard, or foam. Cut them out. (Fig. 1, 2)

STEP 2: Cut a small rectangular slit in the back of the fish's tail.

STEP 3: Add a few inches (cms) of water to a pan or cookie sheet. (Fig. 3)

STEP 4: Place a fish or two in the water on one end of the pan, in head-first racing position. Immediately place a drop of liquid dish detergent in the slot in the fish's tail. (Fig. 4, 5)

STEP 5: Add fresh water to the pan to repeat the experiment.

Fig. 1: Draw fish on paper, cardboard, or foam.

Fig. 2: Cut out the fish shapes.

Fig. 3: Pour a little water into a rectangular dish or pan.

THE SCIENCE
BEHIND THE FUN:

Water molecules like to stick together. On the surface of a liquid, they stick very tightly to their neighboring water molecules, but not as tightly to the air molecules above them. This causes the phenomenon known as surface tension, which forms sort of a liquid "skin" on the water.

You can observe the forces of surface tension at work by dripping water onto a penny, or floating a dense metal needle on the surface of a bowl of water.

When you add detergent to water, it weakens the bonds between the molecules on the surface, breaking the surface tension. In this experiment, the detergent you drip in the slot of the fish tail breaks the surface tension in that small area, and the fish moves as the result of surface tension forces in the soap-free water.

Eventually, the detergent will be dispersed through all the water and you'll have to replace the soapy water to repeat the experiment.

Fig. 4: Put the fish in the water, facing the far end of the pan.

CREATIVE
ENRICHMENT

Try your hand at engineering the perfect zooming fish. What materials work best? How does foil work, or a leaf? Are there other materials you can use to break the surface tension?

MARKER CHROMATOGRAPHY

MATERIALS

→ White coffee filters or paper towels

→ Washable, felt-tip markers

→ Clear glass

→ Water

SEPARATE OUT SOM OF THE COLORFUL DYES THAT MAKE UP MARKER INK.

Fig. 3: Wait for the water to separate the colors as it moves up the filter.

PROTOCOL

STEP 1: Cut paper towels or coffee filters into long strips ¼ inch (6 mm) wide.

STEP 2: Draw a heavy dot or line with one of your markers around ½ inch (1.3 cm) from the bottom of one of the paper strips. Repeat with several colors on several different strips of paper. Be sure to include black, brown, and green. It's fun to make a single dot with lots of different colors to see what happens. (Fig. 1)

STEP 3: Add a little water to the glass.

STEP 4: Put the paper strips into the glass so that the ink dot at one end is just above the water. Once the water starts moving up the paper, it will stick to the side of the glass. You can hook it over the lip of the glass if you want to. (Fig. 2)

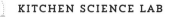

Fig. 1: Draw different-colored dots or lines near the bottom of each paper strip.

Fig. 2: Put the paper strips in water with marker lines and dots just above the water line.

Fig. 4: Use your paper strips for an art project, or tape them into your science notebook.

STEP 5: Wait for the water to separate the colors. Dry the strips and tape them into your science notebook, or use them for an art project. (Fig. 3, 4)

STEP 6: Another fun option is to draw marker dots on paper towels or intact coffee filters, set them on top of a glass jar, and then drip water on the dots with a dropper or straw to make the colors separate out in a circle.

THE SCIENCE
BEHIND THE FUN:

Using water to separate the colors in ink from one another on the paper is a type of liquid chromatography.

When you put the end of a paper strip in water, water molecules travel up the paper towel to wet the dry part above. When the water reaches the ink, it dissolves some of the dyes in the ink, and these dyes travel up the paper with the water molecules. Some of the dye molecules are small and travel up the paper faster than larger dye molecules, so you see the different colors in the ink separate out from one another. The colors you see represent some of the chemicals that make up the color of the marker.

CREATIVE
ENRICHMENT

Try using white vinegar or window cleaner instead of water to carry your pigments up the paper. Does it look the same?

RAINBOW IN A CUP

MATERIALS

→ About 2 cups (480 ml) hot tap water

→ Measuring cups and measuring spoons

→ Jars or drinking cups

→ 20 tablespoons (1 ¼ cups [260 g]) white granulated sugar

→ Food coloring

→ Tall, thin glass (such as a cordial glass) or test tube

→ Eyedropper, siphoning bulb, straw, or spoon

SAFETY
TIPS & HINTS

Use caution with hot liquids.

Add the layers to the cup very slowly and carefully or they'll mix together, resulting in a muddled rainbow.

EXPLORE THE CONCEPT OF DENSITY GRADIENTS BY LAYERING A SUGAR-WATER RAINBOW.

Fig. 5: Complete your liquid rainbow.

PROTOCOL

STEP 1: Measure ½ cup (120 ml) of hot tap water into each of four jars or drinking cups. You can label your cups "2 tablespoons/red," "4 tablespoons/yellow," "6 tablespoons/green," and "8 tablespoons/blue." (Fig. 1)

STEP 2: Add 2 drops of food coloring to each jar, according to the colors they've bee labeled with. (Fig. 2)

STEP 3: To the first cup of hot water, add 2 tablespoons (26 g) of sugar.

STEP 4: To the second jar of hot water, add 4 tablespoons (52 g) of sugar.

STEP 5: To the third jar of hot water, add 6 tablespoons (78 g) of sugar. (Fig. 3)

STEP 6: To the fourth cup of hot water, add 8 tablespoons (104 g) of sugar. By dissolving increasing amounts of sugar, you're increasing the density of the sugar-water solutions.

STEP 7: Stir each of the jars until the sugar dissolves. If the sugar won't dissolve, an adult may microwave the jar for 30 seconds and stir again. Always use caution with h liquids. If the sugar still won't dissolve, try adding a tablespoon (15 ml) of warm water.

Fig. 1: Measure hot tap water into jars
and label.

Fig. 2: Add food coloring, according to
labels.

Fig. 3: Add the correct amount of
sugar to each cup.

Fig. 4: Carefully add each layer,
according to the directions.

STEP 8: Pour about an inch (2.5 cm) of the densest sugar solution (blue) to the bottom of your tall, thin glass or test tube.

STEP 9: Use your dropper or straw to gently drip the liquid with the next-highest density (green) on top of the blue layer. It works best to drip the sugar solution against the side of the cup just above the surface of the liquid. You can also drip it onto the back of a spoon that's set against the side of the cup.

STEP 10: Add the yellow layer in the same way. (Fig. 4)

STEP 11: Complete your rainbow with the red layer, which only contains 2 tablespoons (26 g) of sugar per ½ cup (120 ml) and is the least dense. (Fig. 5)

||| THE SCIENCE
BEHIND THE FUN:

Density is mass (how many atoms are in an object) divided by volume (how much space an object takes up). Sugar molecules are composed of lots of atoms stuck together. The more sugar you add to a ½ cup (120 ml) of water, the more atoms the water will contain and the denser the solution will be. Less dense liquids sit on top of denser liquids, which is why water containing only 2 tablespoons (26 g) of sugar floats on the layers that contain more sugar molecules.

Scientists sometimes use density gradients to isolate different parts of cells by breaking up the cells, putting them on top of a density gradient in a tube and spinning the tube very fast in a centrifuge. Cellular fragments of different shapes and molecular weights move through the gradient at different rates, allowing researchers to separate the cell parts they're interested in studying.

CREATIVE
ENRICHMENT

Can you make a rainbow with more layers? How long will the layers stay separated?

FIREPROOF BALLOON

MATERIALS

→ Balloon

→ Water

→ Lighter or long match

ATTEMPT TO BURN A HOLE IN A WATER BALLOON.

PROTOCOL

STEP 1: Fill a balloon with water and tie it closed. (Fig. 1)

STEP 2: Hold a flame to the bottom of the balloon. (Fig. 2)

STEP 3: See how long it takes to burn through the rubber, or whether it burns through at all.

STEP 4: Optional: Have a water balloon fight. (Fig. 3)

Fig. 1 (above): Fill a balloon with water.

Fig. 2 (left): Hold a flame to the bottom of the baloon.

Fig. 3: Find another way to break your balloon.

THE SCIENCE
BEHIND THE FUN:

Water does more than quench our thirst. In fact, water makes up 60 to 79 percent of our body and plays an essential role in stabilizing our body temperature.

Scientists define specific heat as the amount of heat required to raise the temperature of a substance by 1°C. The specific heat of water is higher than any other common substance, which allows water to absorb and release large quantities of heat with very little change in temperature.

Thanks to its high specific heat, the water in your balloon is able to absorb the heat from the flame and the rubber doesn't melt. Imagine the balloon is a living cell and you can see how the fluid in a cell helps keep it safe when the temperature changes!

What happens if you do this experiment with a frozen water balloon? What happens if you fill a balloon with salt water?

ICE CUBE ON A STRING

MATERIALS

→ Ice cube

→ Glass of room temperature water

→ Cotton kitchen twine or yarn

→ Scissors

→ Salt

LIFT AN ICE CUBE FROM A GLASS USING ONLY A STRING AND SOME SALT.

Fig. 1: Cut a piece of kitchen twine.

PROTOCOL

STEP 1: Cut a piece of kitchen twine about 6 inches (15 cm) long. Drop a few ice cubes into a glass of water. (Fig. 1, 2)

STEP 2: Try to pick the ice cube up by simply placing the string on top of it and pulling. Hint: Don't try too hard, because it won't work.

STEP 3: Dip the string in the water to wet it, lay it across the ice cube, and sprinkle a generous amount of salt over the string/ice cube. (Fig. 3)

STEP 4: Wait a minute or two and try again to lift the cube using only the string. This time, it should work.

Fig. 2: Drop a few ice cubes into a glass of water.

Fig. 3: Sprinkle a big pinch or two of salt on the wet string sitting on an ice cube.

THE SCIENCE
BEHIND THE FUN:

Normally, ice melts and water freezes at 32°F (0°C). Adding salt, however, lowers the temperature at which ice can melt and water can freeze.

In this experiment, salt makes the ice surrounding the string begin to melt, stealing heat from the surrounding water. The cold water then refreezes around the string, which allows you to lift it from the water in the glass.

Different chemicals change the freezing point of water. Salt can thaw ice at 15°F (–9°C), but at 0°F (–18°C) it won't do anything. Other deicing chemicals they add to roads can work at much colder temperatures, down to –20°F (–29°C).

CREATIVE
ENRICHMENT

Does this experiment work using sugar? What else could you try?

UNIT
06

POLYMERS, COLLOIDS & MISBEHAVING MATERIALS

THERE ARE LOTS OF INTERESTING MALLEABLE MATERIALS YOU CAN SYNTHESIZE AND EXPERIMENT WITH IN YOUR OWN KITCHEN, AND THIS UNIT SHOWS YOU HOW TO HAVE SOME FUN WITH THEM.

Play with plastic bags. Use milk, laundry soap, and glue to create homemade adhesive and more than one kind of plastic play dough. A gel, such as gelatin, makes delicious wiggly treats, but it's also a special solution called a colloid that makes a super medium for studying diffusion.

Simple cornstarch is much more fun when you add a little water. It makes a crazy non-Newtonian fluid, called a shear-thickening fluid, which gets thicker, or more viscous, when you agitate it. At the opposite end of the non-Newtonian fluid spectrum are shear-thinning fluids that get less thick as you move them around, and you can make fountains of dish soap to see this magical property at work.

Use your imagination to come up with other inventive uses for the materials in these experiments.

MAGIC BAG

MATERIALS

→ Resealable plastic bag (thick freezer bags work best)

→ Water

→ Food coloring

→ Sharp wooden or bamboo skewers

Be careful with the sharp points of the skewers. Small children should be supervised.

This is a good experiment to do outside, over a sink, or over a bowl.

DO YOU THINK A BAG OF WATER WILL LEAK IF YOU STAB IT WITH A SHARP STICK? THINK AGAIN.

Fig. 2: Push a wooden skewer in one side of the bag and out the other, through the liquid.

PROTOCOL

STEP 1: Fill the resealable plastic bag with water.

STEP 2: Add a drop or two of food coloring to the bag and seal it shut. (Fig. 1)

Fig. 1: Add food coloring to water in a resealable plastic bag and seal closed.

Fig. 3: How many skewers can you poke through your bag before it leaks?

EP 3: Slowly poke a wooden or bamboo skewer completely rough the bag, in one side, through the liquid, and out e other side. Avoid pushing it through the part of the bag ntaining air. (Fig. 2)

STEP 4: See how many skewers you can push through before the bag leaks. (Fig. 3)

THE SCIENCE
BEHIND THE FUN:

Plastic is a polymer, made up of long, elastic molecules that form a seal around the spot where the skewer is poking through. This polymer seal prevents the bag from leaking excessively.

CREATIVE
ENRICHMENT

Does this experiment work with other liquids? What if the water is hot, or cold? What happens if you poke one end of your stick through the portion of the bag that contains air?

MAD SCIENTIST'S GREEN SLIME

MATERIALS

→ Bowl

→ White craft glue, such as Elmer's

→ Water

→ Measuring cups and measuring spoons

→ Jar or bowl

→ Spoon

→ Green food coloring

→ 1 cup (235 ml) warm water

→ 1 heaping tablespoon (20 g) powdered laundry detergent containing sodium borate (borax)

SAFETY
TIPS & HINTS

Young children should be supervised for this experiment because the cross-linking solution and goo contain laundry detergent.

To do this project with several children, divide the glue solution into smaller cups and let them add the detergent solution a spoonful at a time.

SYNTHESIZE A SLIMY, RUBBERY POLYMER CONCOCTION FROM GLUE AND LAUNDRY DETERGENT.

Fig. 5: Pull your slime out of the bowl.

PROTOCOL

STEP 1: Mix together equal parts glue and water in a bowl. For example, you could combine 1/3 cup (80 ml) of glue and 1/3 cup (80 ml) of water. Stir.

STEP 2: Add a few drops of green food coloring and stir again. This is your polymer solution. (Fig. 1)

STEP 3: To make the detergent solution, pour the warm water into a jar or bowl. Add a heaping tablespoon of sodium borate detergent to the water. Shake or stir to dissolve as much detergent as possible. (Fig. 2)

STEP 4: Add a teaspoon (5 ml) at a time of the detergent solution to the glue mixture. Stir following each addition. Long strings will begin to form and stick together. Keep adding detergent until the mixture doesn't feel sticky and forms a shiny rubberlike substance. (Fig. 3)

If you add too much detergent solution, your polymer will feel wet. Squish it around with your hands to absorb the extra solution!

Fig, 1: Mix the watered-down glue with a little food coloring.

Fig, 2: Add the sodium borate detergent to water to make a cross-linking solution. Add glue to a bowl for everyone who wants to make slime.

Fig, 3: Add detergent solution to glue mixture, a spoonful at a time, until glue is no longer sticky.

Fig, 4: Roll your slime into a ball or a long snake.

STEP 5: Remove the green slime from the bowl. Roll it into long snakes or form it into bouncy balls. Store the slime in a plastic bag. To make a larger batch, mix equal amounts of glue and water and add as much borax solution as needed. (Fig. 4, 5)

THE SCIENCE
BEHIND THE FUN:

A molecule is the smallest amount of a specific chemical substance that can exist alone, such as H_2O, a single water molecule. Glue is a polymer, which is a long chain of molecules linked together like a bead necklace. In this experiment, the polymer formed by water and glue is called polyvinyl acetate.

The sodium borate solution is called a cross-linking substance, and it makes the glue polymer chains stick to each other. As more and more chains stick together, they can't move around and the goo gets thicker and thicker. Eventually, all the chains are bound together and no more cross-linking solution can be taken up.

CREATIVE
ENRICHMENT

What happens if you don't dilute the glue with water? What if you dilute it more than 1:1?

MATERIALS

FOR MILK GLUE:

→ 1 cup (235 ml) milk

→ 2 bowls

→ ⅓ cup (80 ml) white vinegar

→ Sieve or coffee filter

→ ⅛ teaspoon (0.6 g) baking soda

→ Water (optional)

FOR MILK PLASTIC:

→ 4 cups (946 ml) milk

→ Medium-size pot

→ ¼ cup (60 ml) white vinegar

→ Heatproof spoon

→ Sieve

Fig. 7: Mold your plastic into shapes and let it dry.

THERE'S MORE TO MILK THAN MEETS THE EYE! USE VINEGAR TO TURN IT INTO GLUE OR PLASTIC.

MILK GLUE PROTOCOL

STEP 1: Place the milk in a bowl. Add the vinegar to the milk and stir. (Fig. 1)

STEP 2: Strain the white blobs, called curds, from the liquid using a sieve or coffee filter. Try to squeeze out any excess liquid. Add the curds to a clean bowl. (Fig. 2)

STEP 3: Add the baking soda to the curds and mix well. You will see bubbles as the baking soda reacts with the vinegar. If your glue is too thick, add a little water. Do an art project with your homemade glue. (Fig. 3)

STEP 4: Store unused glue in the refrigerator for up to two days.

MILK PLASTIC PROTOCOL

STEP 1: Place the milk in a medium-size pot and cook over medium heat until hot but not boiling. (Fig. 4)

Fig, 1: Add the vinegar to the milk.

Fig, 2: Strain out the liquid and save the curds.

Fig, 3: Use your glue for an art project.

Fig, 4: Heat the milk until hot, but not boiling.

Fig, 5: Add the vinegar to the milk and stir.

Fig, 6: Strain out the curds and let them cool.

STEP 2: Add the vinegar to the hot milk and stir. Curds will separate out as large, white lumps. (Fig. 5)

STEP 3: Strain the liquid whey from the curds with a sieve and allow the curds to cool. Try to squeeze out any excess liquid. Add the curds to a clean bowl. (Fig. 6)

STEP 4: Squeeze out any remaining liquid and knead the curds until they're smooth.

STEP 5: Mold the curds into shapes, such as animals, or make beads by forming it around toothpicks. (Fig. 7) When your milk plastic is dry, you can paint it.

THE SCIENCE BEHIND THE FUN:

Milk contains a protein called casein, which is a polymer, or a chain of molecules which can bend and move until the plastic hardens.

Casein doesn't mix with acids, and vinegar is an acid that separates milk, causing the fat, minerals and casein protein to form clumps called curds. White glue is made from caseins of milk curds. Cheeses, as you probably already know, are also made from milk curds.

CREATIVE ENRICHMENT

Can you do the same experiment with other acids, such as lemon juice? What happens if you add more baking soda to your glue?

GELATINOUS DIFFUSION

MATERIALS

→ 4 cups (946 ml) water

→ Medium-size pot

→ 4 (1-ounce [28 g]) envelopes plain, unflavored gelatin (from the grocery store)

→ Heatproof spoon

→ Food coloring

→ Clear heatproof containers or petri dishes

→ Drinking straw

→ Toothpick

SAFETY
TIPS & HINTS

Adult supervision is required to boil water and pour the molten gelatin.

CREATE COLORFUL CIRCLES TO EXPAND YOUR UNDERSTANDING OF DIFFUSION.

Fig. 4: Measure your spots eve hour or so to see how fast the food coloring is moving throug the gelatin.

PROTOCOL

STEP 1: Boil the water in a medium-size pot. Add the gelatin to the boiling water. Stir until dissolved. Let cool slightly.

STEP 2: Pour ½ inch (1.3 cm) of liquid gelatin into the bottom of heatproof containers or petri dishes, and allow it to harden. (Fig. 1)

STEP 3: Using a straw, poke several holes around ¼ inch (6 mm) deep in the gelatin. Try to avoid pushing the straw all the way through the gelatin. Remove the gelatin plugs with a toothpick. (Fig. 2)

STEP 4: Add a different-colored drop of food coloring to each hole on a plate. Do th with several plates. (Fig. 3)

STEP 5: Put one or two plates in the refrigerator and leave a few at room temperatur

STEP 6: Every so often, measure the circle of food coloring as it diffuses into the surrounding gelatin. How many centimeters per hour is it diffusing? Does the temperature make a difference? (Fig. 4, 5)

fig. 1: Pour around ½ inch (1.3 cm) of liquid gelatin into several heatproof plates.

fig. 2: Use straws to make holes in the gelatin.

fig. 3: Drop food coloring into each hole.

fig. 5: Does the food coloring diffuse faster at room temperature, or in the refrigerator?

THE SCIENCE
BEHIND THE FUN:

Gelatin is a special substance known as a hydrocolloid, which is a suspension of tiny particles in a water-based solution. It's similar to agar-agar and is a good medium to use for diffusion experiments since it doesn't support another kind of movement in fluids, called convection.

Diffusion is the name for the way molecules move from areas of high concentration, where there are lots of other similar molecules, to areas of low concentration, where there are fewer similar molecules. When the molecules are evenly spread throughout the space, it is called equilibrium. Imagine half a box filled with yellow balls and the other half filled with blue ones. If you set the box on something that vibrates, the balls will start to move around randomly, until the blue and yellow balls are evenly mixed up.

Many things can affect how fast molecules diffuse, including temperature. When molecules are heated up, they vibrate faster and move around faster, which helps them achieve equilibrium more quickly.

Diffusion takes place in gases, liquids, and even solids, which is one way pollutants are able to move from one place to another. Bacteria take up some of the substances they need to survive using simple diffusion across their membranes. Your own body transfers oxygen, carbon dioxide, and water by processes involving diffusion as well.

CREATIVE ENRICHMENT

Do the same experiment, but make plates using 2 cups (475 ml) of red cabbage juice (see Lab 1, "Color-Changing Magic Potion"), 2 cups (475 ml) of water and 4 (1-ounce [28 g]) envelopes of gelatin. See how fast a few drops of vinegar or baking soda and water solution diffuse. A pigment in red cabbage turns pink when exposed to acid, and blue/green when exposed to a base!

CORNSTARCH GOO

MATERIALS

→ Medium-size bowl

→ Spoon (optional)

→ 1 cup + 2 tablespoons (147 g) cornstarch

→ ½ cup (120 ml) water

→ Food coloring (optional for colored goo)

Food coloring will move from the goo to hands and clothes, so beware.

For colored goo, simply add the food coloring to the water before mixing with cornstarch.

Without food coloring, this project cleans up easily with water.

MIX UP A BATCH OF NON-NEWTONIAN FUN.

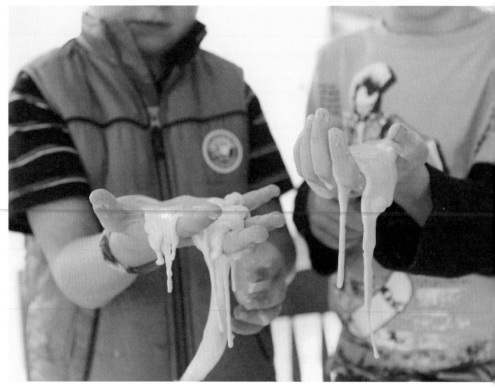

Fig. 5: What happens if you stop moving it around?

PROTOCOL

STEP 1: Mix together the cornstarch, water, and food coloring in a medium-size bowl using a spoon or your fingers. The goo should be the consistency of thick syrup. (Fig. 1, 2, 3)

STEP 2: Remove some goo from the bowl and roll it into a ball. (Fig. 4)

STEP 3: Stop rolling it and let it drip between your fingers. (Fig. 5)

Fig. 1: Add the water to the cornstarch.

Fig. 2: Stir your cornstarch and water to mix.

Fig. 3: Add a little bit of food coloring to your goo.

Fig. 4: Roll the goo into a ball between your palms.

STEP 4: Put the goo on a tray or cookie sheet. What happens if you slap your hand down on it? Can you make it splash?

STEP 5: If the goo gets too dry, just add a little more water.

THE SCIENCE
BEHIND THE FUN:

Most fluids and solids behave in expected ways and hold their fluid or solid properties when you push, pull, squeeze, pour, or shake them. However, some fluids, known as non-Newtonian fluids, don't follow the rules. Cornstarch goo is one of these renegade fluids. It's called a shear-thickening non-Newtonian fluid, and when you apply stress to it, the atoms in the cornstarch rearrange to make it act more like a solid.

That's why when you let the goo sit in the palm of your hand or let it slowly slide between your fingers it looks like liquid, but if you squeeze it, stir it, or roll it around in your hands, it looks and feels more like a solid.

Someday, fluids such as these may be used to make such things as bulletproof vests that will move with the wearer but stop speeding projectiles.

CREATIVE
ENRICHMENT

What happens if you add more or less water? Does it retain the same properties? Can you think of some practical uses for non-Newtonian fluids?

MATERIALS

→ Chair

→ Tape

→ Liquid hand soap

→ Resealable plastic bag

→ Large plate or pan

→ Scissors

→ 1 mm pastry tip (optional [see note])

SAFETY
TIPS & HINTS

Before you start, see the resources section on page 141 for a link to a video of the Kaye effect so you can see how it should look once you get it set up perfectly.

Like a real scientist, you'll have to experiment with several variables for optimal results. The type of soap you use, the size of the hole you cut, and the height of the bag will all have to be optimized before you'll see the shooting jets of soap.

Fig. 5: Some of the soap jets will last for a second or two.

TEST YOUR EXPERIMENTAL SKILLS AS YOU MAKE AMAZING MINI-FOUNTAINS FROM LIQUID SOAP.

PROTOCOL

STEP 1: Fill a resealable plastic bag about halfway with liquid soap or dish detergent. Add a few drops of food coloring. (Fig. 1)

STEP 2: Tape the bag to a chair, with one corner of the bag pointed toward a plate underneath. Try starting with the bag 24 inches (61 cm) above the plate. (Fig. 2)

STEP 3: With scissors, cut off the corner of the bag closest to the floor, to make a tiny hole (1 mm) for the soap to flow through. You may have to make it a little bigger, but you want a very thin, steady stream of soap flowing to the plate. (Fig. 3)

STEP 4: Look for jumping fountains of soap where the soap piles up under the stream. (Fig. 4, 5)

Note: The physicist who gave me the idea for this experiment used a 1 mm pastry tip in his plastic bag and hung the bag around 8 inches (20 cm) above the plate. (See Resources on page 141.)

Fig. 1: Add some liquid hand soap to a resealable plastic bag.

2: Tape the bag of soap to a
air, with one corner pointing
aight down.

*Fig. 3: Cut a very tiny hole by clipping
the corner of the plastic bag.*

4: Look for fountains jumping from the pile of soap under the stream.

Ketchup, no drip paint, liquid soaps, and shampoos are all part of an amazing category of non-Newtonian fluids known as shearing liquids. These fluids are fairly thick when they're sitting still, but they become more "liquidy" as they flow, because movement decreases their viscosity, or thickness, making them more slippery. Shearing has to do with both speed and direction.

In 1963, an engineer named Arthur Kaye noticed streams of liquid shooting from the surface below a stream of shearing liquid he was working with. This strange phenomenon became known as the Kaye effect.

CREATIVE
ENRICHMENT

What happens if you position the plate below the bag at an angle?

UNIT
07

ACIDS & BASES

IN THIS UNIT, WE'LL USE PLANT PIGMENTS TO EXPLORE ACIDITY.

Compounds called acids and bases are polar opposites when you dissolve them in water. While acids dissolve in water to release positively charged hydrogen ions (protons), bases take up these protons or donate negatively charged ions to the solution. Scientists made up the pH scale as a way to specify the acidity or alkalinity of a solution, depending on how many protons are around. The scale goes from very acidic, at a pH of 0, to very basic (alkaline) at a pH of 14.

Water has about the same number of protons and hydroxyl ions, so it has a neutral pH of around 7. The pH of the hydrochloric acid in your stomach is about 1, pickles have a pH of a little more than 3, and household bleach has a pH between 9 and 10.

Many scientists use special paper treated with certain plant pigments to test the pH of solutions. Pigments are molecules that give things color, and certain pigments are acid/base indicators. That means that they change color when you expose them to different pHs. The first litmus paper was made from lichens, but you can make your own with red cabbage and coffee filters.

RED CABBAGE LITMUS PAPER

MATERIALS

→ Head of red cabbage

→ Medium-size pot

→ Water

→ Heatproof spoon

→ White coffee filters or paper towels

→ Scissors

SAFETY
TIPS & HINTS

An adult should chop and boil the red cabbage. When the juice is cool, kids can take over.

Note: To avoid needing to use the stove, chop half a head of red cabbage and blend in a blender with about 3 cups (710 ml) of water. Strain the liquid through a colander and then through a coffee filter in a plastic bag with one corner cut off.

MAKE ART-WORTHY ACID/BASE INDICATOR PAPER WITH RED CABBAGE AND COFFEE FILTERS.

Fig. 4: Dip your paper in the vinegar, soap, lemon juice, and baking soda solution.

PROTOCOL

STEP 1: Chop half a head of red cabbage into small pieces and place it in a pot. Cover with water. (Fig. 1) Boil the cabbage uncovered for about 15 minutes, stirring occasionally.

STEP 2: When juice is cool, strain it into a jar or bowl.

STEP 3: Soak paper towels or coffee filters in the cabbage juice for a few minutes. (F

STEP 4: Remove the filters or paper towels and let them dry on something that won' stain. You can blot them to speed up the drying process. For more intense color, repe soaking/drying step. When they're dry, cut the filters or paper towels into strips aroun ¾ inch (2 cm) wide. (Fig. 3)

Fig. 1: Chop a head of red cabbage.

Fig. 2: Soak white coffee filters or paper towels in red cabbage juice.

Fig. 3: Cut the cabbage-stained paper into strips to use as litmus paper.

STEP 6: When dry, your litmus paper will be ready to use. Dip the paper into soapy water, lemon juice, baking soda in water, baking powder in water, white vinegar, and anything else you want to test. The paper will turn red-pink in acidic solutions and blue or green in basic solutions. (Fig. 4, 5)

Fig. 5: Your paper will turn pink in acids and blue in bases.

THE SCIENCE
BEHIND THE FUN:

Acid molecules dissolve in water and break apart, releasing free-floating hydrogen ions called protons. When bases are dissolved in water, they also break apart, but they form ions that want to react with acids and take up hydrogen ions.

The molecules in the cabbage juice that give it color are called pigments, and the pigments in red cabbage juice are special molecules called acid-base indicators. Depending on whether they're exposed to an acid or base, they change shape slightly. This causes them to absorb light differently and change color. That's why, when you expose red cabbage juice litmus paper to an acid, it turns red or pink, and when you expose it to a base, it turns green or blue.

CREATIVE
ENRICHMENT

Use the remaining cabbage juice for another experiment, such as Lab 1 "Color-Changing Magic Potion," Lab 26 "Gelatinous Diffusion" enrichment, or Lab 30 "Ocean Acidification Experiment."

OCEAN ACIDIFICATION EXPERIMENT

MATERIALS

→ Head of red cabbage

→ Knife

→ Medium-size pot

→ Water

→ Carbonated water

→ Heatproof spoon

→ Colander lined with a paper coffee filter (optional [see note])

→ Small clear or white cups or test tubes

→ Drinking straws (optional)

USE RED CABBAGE JUICE, CARBONATED WATER, AND YOUR BREATH TO VISUALIZE ACIDIFICATION BY CARBON DIOXIDE.

Fig. 3: Carbon dioxide acidifies the cabbage juice, making it turn pinker.

PROTOCOL

STEP 1: Chop half a head of red cabbage into small pieces and place it in a pot. Cove with water. Boil the cabbage uncovered for about 15 minutes, stirring occasionally.

STEP 2: When juice is cool, strain it into a jar or bowl.

STEP 3: Pour a few teaspoons (about 10 ml) of the red cabbage juice into each of tw small cups or test tubes.

STEP 4: Add carbonated water to one cup of cabbage juice and tap water to the oth cup of cabbage juice. Try to add about the same volume of water or carbonated wate to each cup, and for a better control, use carbonated water and noncarbonated water from the same source, or use dry ice to carbonate water. (Fig. 1)

STEP 5: Observe any color change. Red cabbage juice turns pink when exposed to a acid and blue when exposed to a base. (Fig. 2, 3)

STEP 6: (Optional) Repeat step 1 by pouring 1 or 2 ml of red cabbage juice into each of two small cups or test tubes. Take a straw, put it all the way against the bottom of one cup, and blow through the straw for several minutes until you see the cabbage juice turn pinker than the juice in the control cup. Be patient! Test tubes are less mess because the juice can't splatter as much. (Fig. 4, 5)

Fig. 1: Add noncarbonated water to one glass of cabbage juice and carbonated water to the other.

Fig. 2: Observe the color change.

Fig. 4: Blow through a straw into a small volume of cabbage juice.

Note: To avoid needing to use the stove, make red cabbage juice by chopping half a head of red cabbage and blending it with about 3 cups (710 ml) of water. Strain the liquid through a colander and then through a coffee filter inside a plastic bag with one corner cut off. Uncooked cabbage juice makes longer-lasting bubbles and turns a slightly brighter shade of blue.

Fig. 5: The carbon dioxide in your breath will make the cabbage juice slightly pinker.

THE SCIENCE
BEHIND THE FUN:

The pigment in red cabbage is an acid indicator and turns red or pink in the presence of acid. The carbon dioxide that makes bubbles in carbonated water, or the carbon dioxide in your breath, combines with the water in the cabbage juice to form carbonic acid, causing the pH of the solution to drop and the cabbage juice to turn pink.

A large percentage of the carbon dioxide released by human activities, such as burning fossil fuels and burning rainforests, is absorbed by our world's oceans. This results in the ocean's water becoming more acidic, like the cabbage juice in the experiment. This drop in pH along with other changes in ocean chemistry makes it hard for some sea life, such as coral, to survive and reproduce.

You can also imagine why the carbon dioxide in drinking soda makes it acidic and bad for your teeth.

CREATIVE
ENRICHMENT

What color will cabbage juice turn if you add yeast and let it grow for a while? Try doing Lab 33, "Yeast Balloons", using cabbage juice instead of water.

Pour colorless soda into red cabbage juice to see what happens.

SPY JUICE

MATERIALS

→ 2 cups (200 g) whole fresh cranberries

→ Knife

→ Medium-size lidded pot

→ 3 ⅓ cups (710 ml) water, plus more for step 7, if needed

→ Sieve or colander

→ Casserole dish or baking pan large enough to hold a sheet of paper

→ Baking soda

→ ⅓ cup (80 ml) warm water

→ All-purpose printer paper

→ Scissors

→ Cotton swabs, paintbrushes, or cake-pop sticks

→ Lemon juice (optional)

REVEAL INVISIBLE MESSAGES USING THE ACID/BASE-SENSITIVE PIGMENTS IN CRANBERRIES.

Fig. 5: Reveal your message with cranberry juice.

SAFETY TIPS & HINTS

Boiling the berries should be done by an adult. Keep the lid on the pot because the air pockets that make cranberries float can also make them explode. Kids can take over once the juice is cool.

You may have to try more than one kind of paper. There are instructions for testing your paper in the protocol.

A cake-pop stick or a cotton swab with the ends cut off make the best pens to use with the "invisible ink" in this experiment.

PROTOCOL

STEP 1: Cut a cranberry in half and observe the air pockets that make it float. (Fig. 1)

STEP 2: Boil the cranberries in 3 cups (710 ml) of the water for 15 to 20 minutes, covered. Listen for popping sounds as the air in the cranberries heats up and they explode. (Fig. 2, 3)

STEP 3: To collect the concentrated cranberry juice, crush the cooked berries and push the liquid through a sieve or colander into a casserole dish or pan that is big enough to hold a piece of paper.

STEP 4: Allow the juice to cool. If your cranberry juice seems thick and syrupy, add a little water so that it's thin enough to soak into paper!

Fig. 1: Cut some cranberries in half to see the air pockets inside.

Fig. 2: Add the water to the cranberries.

Fig. 3: Cover and cook the cranberries.

Fig. 4: Write messages on the paper.

STEP 5: Test the paper you want to use by cutting a small piece and soaking it in the cranberry juice. If it stays pink, it will work, but if it turns blue or gray immediately, try some other paper.

STEP 6: Make invisible ink by adding a few teaspoons (about 9 g) of baking soda to ⅓ cup (80 ml) of warm water and stir well. Don't worry if you can still see some baking soda. You can also write messages with lemon juice.

STEP 7: With a pen made from cotton swab, paintbrush, or cake-pop stick, use the baking soda solution and/or lemon juice as ink to write a message on your paper. It may take a little practice. (Fig. 4) Let your message air dry, or speed things up with a blow dryer.

STEP 8: To reveal your message, place your paper in the cranberry juice and see what happens! (Fig. 5)

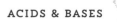

THE SCIENCE
BEHIND THE FUN:

Cranberries contain pigments called anthocyanins (an-tho-SY-a-nins) that give them their bright color. In nature, these pigments attract birds and other animals to fruit.

These pigments, called flavanoids, change color when they come in contact with acids and bases. Cranberry juice is very acidic, and the pigment is pink in acids, but when you add it to a base, it turns purple or blue.

Baking soda is a base, so your baking soda message will turn blue when it comes into contact with the pigments in the cranberry juice. Eventually, when enough cranberry juice soaks into the paper, it will dilute the baking soda, turning the pigment back to red and your message will disappear!

There are over three hundred kinds of anthocyanins, which are found in many fruits and vegetables. Scientists believe they may have many health benefits.

CREATIVE
ENRICHMENT

What other natural acid/base indicators could you use to do this experiment? What else could you use as ink?

MARVELOUS MICROBIOLOGY

FROM THE TIME WE'RE BORN, TINY CREATURES LAY CLAIM TO ALMOST EVERY EXPOSED CENTIMETER OF OUR BODY. TOO SMALL TO SEE WITH THE NAKED EYE, SOME OF THEM CAN MAKE YOU SICK BUT MANY ARE ESSENTIAL TO HUMAN HEALTH.

Like most living things, microorganisms are particular about where they grow and what they need to survive. Although some thrive at body temperature and can live on the nutrients provided by human skin, others prefer to live under different conditions. Some bacteria, called extremophiles, can live in environments that are too hot, cold, acidic, or radioactive for most things to survive. Fascinating nonliving microbes called viruses can only make new copies of themselves by hijacking living cells and stealing their machinery.

To grow microbes in a lab, researchers must provide optimal environments for their growth. Most microbes are grown in nutrient broth or on solid growth medium plates. Nutrient broth allows for the growth of large numbers of bacteria, while solid agar plates, like the ones you can make in this unit, allow for the isolation of individual microbes.

A tiny percentage of the bacteria and fungi in the environment and on your skin will grow readily at room temperature. In this chapter, you'll have the opportunity to explore what microbes are growing around your house, observe how yeast makes bread rise, and learn why it's so important to wash your hands with soap and water.

HOMEMADE PETRI PLATE AND MICROBE ZOOS

MATERIALS

→ Clean, disposable containers, such as individual foil muffin tins or clear plastic cups covered with resealable plastic bags, clear plastic ware with lids, or petri dishes

→ Small pot or microwavable bowl

→ Beef bouillon cubes or 1 teaspoon (about 2 g) granules

→ 1 cup (235 ml) water

→ 1 tablespoon (14 g) powdered agar-agar or 1 ½ envelopes (0.5-ounce [12 g]) unflavored gelatin (see note)

→ 2 teaspoons (9 g) sugar

→ Plate or plastic wrap

→ Cotton swabs

→ Pen and labels

SAFETY TIPS & HINTS

Making the plates requires handling very hot liquids, so adult assistance is required.

If you use foil muffin cups as your petri dishes, simply place them in a muffin pan, fill them with agar-agar, and when they're cool, put them in individual resealable plastic bags.

Plates should be used in two to three days. When you're working with them, try to keep the lids on loosely whenever possible, so that they're not contaminated by microorganisms floating around in the air.

Wash your hands after handling the plates, and throw them away when you're finished observing them.

WHAT'S ON YOUR KITCHEN COUNTER? GROW COLONIES FROM SOME OF THE MICROBES LIVING AROUND YOUR HOME.

Fig. 4: See what grows!

PROTOCOL

STEP 1: To make the microbe food, or microbial growth medium, mix the beef bouillon, water, agar-agar or gelatin, and sugar together in a small pot or microwavable bowl. (Fig. 1)

STEP 2: Bring the mixture to a boil on the stove, stirring at 1-minute intervals and watching carefully until the agar-agar or gelatin is dissolved. Remove boiling liquid from the heat and cover with a plate or plastic wrap. Let cool for about 15 minutes.

STEP 3: Pour the medium carefully into the clean containers, about one-third full. Loosely place lids, or plastic bags over the containers and allow them to cool completely. When the portions of the mixture are solid, they're ready to use or store (sealed) in a refrigerator. (Fig. 2)

Fig. 1: Mix together ingredients.

Fig. 2: Pour plates.

Fig. 3: Take samples by swabbing surfaces.

STEP 4: Shake the condensation (water droplets) off the lids of the containers and replace the lids. Label the bottom of each container with the date and name of the surface you want to test. Use a separate container for each surface or divide each plate into four sections and label each section.

STEP 5: Test surfaces by rubbing a clean cotton swab around on the surface you want to test. Remove the lid from the container labeled with the name of that surface and gently rub the swab across the section of the plate labeled for that surface. Phones, remote controls, kitchen sinks, computer keyboards, doorknobs, and piano keys are great surfaces to check. You can even touch your finger to the plate, cough on a plate, or leave one open to the air for half an hour to see what's floating around. (Fig. 3)

STEP 7: When you're done swabbing, set the plates on a flat surface with their lids loosened and taped on.

STEP 8: Observe your plates to see what grows. You'll mostly see fungi (molds), but you may also see some tiny clear or white spots that are colonies formed by millions of bacteria. (Fig. 4) Note the shapes, sizes, and colors of the microbial colonies that grow on your plates.

Note: Gelatin will melt if it gets too warm, and some strains of bacteria can liquefy it, which is why scientists in labs use agar-agar to make their plates. Agar-agar is made from algae and can be found in the Asian food section of many grocery stores.

THE SCIENCE
BEHIND THE FUN:

Although you can't see them without a microscope, microbes, such as fungi and bacteria, live on your body and every surface you see around you. Some of them can be grown on the microbial growth media in this experiment. Like animals in a zoo, each microbe has its own particular requirements for food, moisture, temperature, and even how much air it gets. The colonies you grow must use the food and temperature you provide for them.

Colony size, color, and other characteristics can help identify what's growing on your plates. Microbiologists use microscopy, staining, chemical tests, and even nucleic acid analysis to identify unknown organisms.

CREATIVE
ENRICHMENT

What other experiments could you do with your petri plates? Try Lab 34, "The Hand-Washing Experiment."

LAB 33 YEAST BALLOONS

MATERIALS

→ Small resealable plastic bags

→ Pen

→ 4 (2 ¼ -teaspoon [9 g]) packages active dry yeast

→ 1 teaspoon (6 g) salt

→ 6 teaspoons (27 g) sugar

→ 2 cups (475 ml) water

Fig. 3: Add sugar to the bags you've labeled "Sugar."

MAKE YEAST BALLOONS TO DISCOVER WHAT MAKES YEAST GROW.

PROTOCOL

STEP 1: Label four resealable plastic bag as follows:

"Sugar + warm water"

"Sugar + cold water"

"Sugar + salt + warm water"

"No sugar + warm water" (Fig. 1)

STEP 2: Add 4 (2 ¼ -teaspoon (9 g]) packages of yeast to each plastic bag. Add 2 teaspoons (9 g) of sugar to each of the three bags labeled "Sugar," and the salt to the bag labeled "Salt." (Fig. 2, 3)

STEP 3: Carefully, add ½ cup (120 ml) of water to each bag, according to how each ba is labeled. The warm water should be warm, but not too hot, or it will kill the yeast. Th cold water can be room temperature, or you can chill it with ice. (Fig. 4)

SAFETY
TIPS & HINTS

Keep an eye on your experiment. If one of the bags looks as if it might explode, open it to let the pressure out!

Fig. 1: Label your plastic bags.

Fig. 2: Add yeast to each bag.

g. 4: Add water to each bag.

TEP 4: Seal the
ags, squeezing out
much of the extra
r as possible and let
em sit. Yeast will
ow faster in a warm
om than in a cold
e.

TEP 5: Watch the
ags to see what
appens. You will
ow your yeast cells
e growing happily
the bag containing
em puffs up as
rbon dioxide gas
cumulates. (Fig. 5)

Sugar + salt + warm water

Sugar + warm water

No sugar + warm water

Sugar + cold water

Fig. 5: What makes the yeast grow best?

'hich ingredients help yeast grow best? Did you find an ingredient
at kept them from growing well? Do yeast cells grow better in
arm or cold water?

Humans have been making bread for over four
thousand years. How bread rose was a mystery
though, until a famous scientist named Louis Pasteur
proved that tiny living organisms called yeast were
responsible for making bread dough puff up.

Bread yeast is a type of fungus related to mushrooms.
If you look at yeast cells under a microscope, you'll see
that they're shaped like balloons and footballs. The
yeast used to make bread is called *Saccharomyces
cerevisiae* (sack-a-roe-MY-seas sair-a-VIS-e-ey).
Saccharomyces means "sugar fungus."

Growing yeast cells use sugar and starches, such as
the ones in bread flour, for energy. Sugar and starch-
eating yeast cells produce carbon dioxide gas, which
is what makes your plastic bag puff up.

In bread dough, carbon dioxide gas from yeast makes
tiny bubbles that make the bread rise. They pop
during baking, but leave the small holes you see in
bread. The yeast you buy at the store is alive, but it is
dried and can't grow until you add water to it.

CREATIVE ENRICHMENT

Try coating the yeast with oil before adding
the sugar and water. What happens if you add fruit
juice to the bags? What if you put the bags in the
refrigerator just after adding the yeast?

HAND-WASHING EXPERIMENT

MATERIALS

→ Six homemade petri plates from Lab 32

→ Pen and labels

→ Clean towel

→ Clean bar or liquid soap

→ Alcohol-based hand sanitizer

Fig. 2: Wash your fingers with water alone.

DISCOVER THE BEST WAY TO REMOVE DISEASE-CAUSING MICROBES FROM YOUR HANDS.

PROTOCOL

STEP 1: Label the bottom of each of six plates A through F, as follows:

"A": Right hand: no washing

"B": Right hand: water alone

"C": Right hand: soap and water

"D": Right hand: hand sanitizer

"E": Control plate: untouched

Be sure to include the date and your initials on the plate as well. (Fig. 1)

STEP 2: Quickly remove the lid from plate A and, with the four fingertips on your right hand, gently touch the growth medium, as if to leave fingerprints. Replace the lid.

STEP 3: Wash the same four fingers with water and no scrubbing for about 30 seconds, blot dry with a clean towel, and touch plate B as in Step 2. (Fig. 2, 3, 4)

STEP 4: Scrub the same four fingers on your right hand with soap and water for 2 minutes, blot with a clean towel and touch plate C.

STEP 5: Scrub your right hand with hand sanitizer for about 30 seconds. Touch plate D.

SAFETY
TIPS & HINTS

Adults must assist in making petri plates and should supervise young children when using hand sanitizer.

STEP 6: Tape down the lids on your plates, put them somewhere out of the way and check them after a few days. Soon you should see bacterial and fungal colonies begin to appear.

STEP 8: Count the colonies on each of your plates. How do they compare?

Fig. 1: Make the petri plates from Lab 32 and label them.

Fig. 3: Blot your fingers dry on a clean towel.

Fig. 4: Touch the plate labeled "water alone."

THE SCIENCE BEHIND THE FUN:

Scrubbing your hands with soap, rinsing them well with clean water, and rubbing them dry on a clean towel can significantly reduce the number of disease-causing germs on your fingertips. Hand-washing is one of the best ways to avoid catching and spreading infectious diseases. Hand sanitizer is effective at killing many microbes, but some are resistant and can only be killed or physically removed by scrubbing and rinsing. Soap also helps break up the oils on your hands, allowing better removal.

This experiment lets you grow colonies from some of the bacteria and fungi on your hands, illustrating how washing with soap helps get your hands clean. Bacterial colonies will appear as small clear, white, and yellow dots on your plates.

Microbes called residents are always on your skin. Others, such as many disease-causing germs, are called transient. You pick up transient microbes on surfaces everywhere, but drinking fountain handles, stairwell railings, and computer keyboards are especially notorious for harboring these germs. The friction involved in rubbing your hands together while washing and rinsing is the most important aspect of removing these transient microbes.

Doctors, nurses, and people who work with food have to be especially careful about hand-washing so they don't spread disease in the workplace.

CREATIVE ENRICHMENT

Do this experiment and compare a heavily used bar of soap to liquid soap. Which leaves your hands cleaner?

Do Lab 32, "Homemade Petri Plates and Microbe Zoos," to see which surfaces in your home harbor the most microbes.

SHOCKING SCIENCE

HAVE YOU EVER GOTTEN A SHOCK FROM A DOORKNOB AFTER SHUFFLING ACROSS A CARPET?

The term static electricity refers to the buildup of a positive or negative electrical charge on the surface of an object. In the case of the rug and the doorknob, the charged object is your body. You feel an electric shock as the charge you've collected from the carpet jumps from your hand to the metal doorknob.

Tiny sub-atomic particles with negative charges are called electrons. They can jump from object to object and play an essential role in the wonders of electricity and magnetism. The positively charged counterparts of electrons are much bigger and heavier and are called protons.

Protons and electrons are attracted to each other, due to their unlike charges, but often electrons will do most of the moving, since they're smaller and lighter.

Electrons are repelled by other electrons, since they have the same charge, and will try to avoid each other. The same holds true for protons.

For example, when you rub a balloon on your hair, or a comb through it, many electrons are stripped from your hair and move to the balloon or comb giving it a negative charge. This often leaves your hair standing up as all the positively charged strands physically repel each other.

This unit shows you some fun ways to visualize, and even be shocked by, electrons moving from one object to another.

DANCING FOIL ELECTROSCOPE

MATERIALS

→ Jar

→ Cardboard

→ Scissors

→ Thin aluminum foil or Mylar (the shiny material used to make some balloons and candy wrappers)

→ Nail

→ Tape

→ Balloon or plastic comb

USE STATIC ELECTRICITY TO MOVE FOIL STRIPS IN A JAR, AS IF BY MAGIC.

Fig. 4: Replace the cardboard lid on the jar without disturbing the foil on the nail.

PROTOCOL

STEP 1: Cut a piece of cardboard to fit over the mouth of the jar and place it on the jar.

STEP 2: Poke the nail through the cardboard, point down. Remove the cardboard and nail from the jar, leaving the nail in the cardboard. (Fig. 1, 2)

STEP 3: Cut two strips of foil or Mylar, each 2 inches (5 cm) long and about ¼ inch (6 mm) wide, and lay one on top of the other.

STEP 4: Keeping them together, tape the two strips of foil or Mylar to the pointed tip of the nail and replace the cardboard lid to the jar so the foil strips hang down, just touching each other. (Fig. 3, 4)

STEP 5: Charge a balloon or comb by rubbing it on your hair. (Fig. 5) Bring the charged object close to the nail head. You don't have to touch it.

STEP 6: The foil strips should move away from each other as you move the negatively charged balloon or comb toward the nail. (Fig. 6)

Fig. 1: Push a nail through a piece of cardboard.

Fig. 2: The nail should be long enough to extend down into the jar.

Fig. 3: Tape two thin strips of foil to the tip of the nail so they lie flat against each other.

Fig. 5: (left) Give a balloon or comb a charge by rubbing it on your hair.

Fig. 6: (left) Bring the charged balloon or comb near the nail head and watch the foil strips move.

THE SCIENCE BEHIND THE FUN:

Negatively charged balloons and combs are great tools for making electrons jump around.

In this experiment, negatively charged electrons from your hair jump to the balloon or comb, and then to the nail, and finally into the strips of foil. In addition, the overall negative charge on the balloon pushes even more electrons down to the foil to give both strips a strong negative charge. Objects with similar charges repel each other, so the foil strips push each other away.

CREATIVE ENRICHMENT

What will happen if you use more than two foil strips? Try to make a foil "squid" with lots of legs and see what occurs.

Are there other charged objects you can use to make your foil strips "dance"?

MATERIALS

→ Cardboard square slightly larger than the Styrofoam plate (below)

→ Aluminum pie pan

→ Tape

→ Styrofoam cup

→ Styrofoam plate

→ Aluminum foil

→ Woolen object, such as an old mitten or stocking cap

→ Small container such as a plastic film canister or empty spice container

→ Duct tape

→ Metal nail longer than the canister

→ Water

SAFETY
TIPS & HINTS

An adult should help young children push the nail through the film canister cap.

Once you've made your electrophorus and Leyden jar, it's important to do the steps in order, or the experiment won't work.

TRY THIS STATIC ELECTRICITY EXPERIMENT WITH A SHOCKING CONCLUSION.

Fig. 4: For a shock, touch the foil on the Leyden jar with your thumb and bring a finger on the same hand close to the nail.

STEP 1: Tape the top of the foam cup to the inside of the pie pan.

STEP 2: Cover one side of the cardboard with foil and tape it on underneath. Tape the Styrofoam plate onto the foil, face down.

STEP 3: Fill your small container ¾ full with water. Cap the container with its lid or duct tape. Cover the bottom two-thirds of the container with foil and push the nail through the lid or duct tape so the pointy end is in the water. Use duct tape to hold it in place, if needed. (Fig. 1)

Remember, it's important to do the next steps in order!

STEP 4: Rub the foam plate (that's taped to the foil) with a woolen object for about a minute. Set it plate side up on a flat surface near your Leyden jar. (Fig. 2)

STEP 5: Holding the cup handle, place the pie tin, cup-side-up, on top of the foam plate. (Fig. 3)

STEP 6: Put your pinkie on the foil covering the cardboard and leave it there while you touch the pie tin with the thumb on the same hand. You might feel a small spark as the electrons jump from the pie plate to your hand. Now the pie plate has a positive charge. (Fig. 4)

STEP 7: Using the foam cup, lift the charged pie tin and touch it to the head of the nail on your Leyden jar. Electrons will flow from the nail to the pie plate, leaving the nail and inside of the jar with a positive charge. (Fig. 5)

STEP 8: Repeat steps 1 through 3 two or three times to build up a charge in your Leyden jar.

STEP 9: When you're ready for a shock, put your thumb on the foil on the bottom of your Leyden jar, leave it there, and bring your fingertip close to the nail on the jar. Electrons will jump from the foil on the bottom of the Leyden jar to the positively charged nail, giving you a shock. (Fig. 6)

Fig. 1: Add water to your Leyden jar.

Fig. 2: Rub the foam plate with wool.   *Fig. 3: Place the pie tin on the foam plate.*

Fig. 4: Put your pinkie on the foil and touch the pie tin with your thumb.   *Fig. 5: Touch the pie tin to the nail on the Leyden jar.*

THE SCIENCE
BEHIND THE FUN:

An electrophorus is a simple device used to produce electrostatic charge.

When you rub the foam plate with wool, the Styrofoam attracts electrons from the wool, giving it a negative charge. Touching the pie tin to the charged foam plate causes the electrons on the pie tin to be repelled by the negative charge on the foam plate, but they have nowhere to go. When you touch the foil and then the pie plate, your fingers create a bridge for the repelled electrons and they jump from the pie plate to your hand, leaving the pie plate with a positive charge. A Leyden jar stores static electricity between two electrodes on the inside and outside of a container. Our film canister's jar has an inside electrode of water, and an outside electrode made of foil.

Touching the positively charged pie plate to the head of the nail on your Leyden jar allows electrons to flow from the water and the nail to the pie plate, leaving the nail and the water inside the jar with a positive charge.

In the final step of the experiment, when you touch the foil on the bottom of your Leyden jar and then move your fingertip toward the negatively charged nail, a stream of electrons jumps from the foil on the bottom of the jar to the positively charged nail, giving you a shock.

CREATIVE ENRICHMENT

Try the final step in the dark. You may see a spark as the electrons move through the air to your finger.

WATER BENDER

MATERIALS

→ Latex balloons

→ Pin

→ Plastic comb

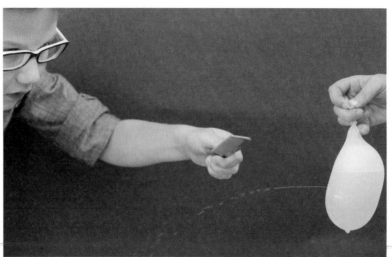

USE STATIC ELECTRICITY TO BEND A STREAM OF WATER.

Fig. 2: Bring the comb close to the stream of water.

PROTOCOL

STEP 1: Fill a balloon with water until it's about halfway full. Do not overfill.

STEP 2: Tie the balloon closed.

STEP 3: Put a small hole in the side of the balloon with a pin so a thin stream of water comes out when you hold it by the tie on top. (Fig. 1)

STEP 4: Charge a comb by running it through your hair a number of times. Your hair must be dry.

STEP 5: Hold the comb next to the stream of water coming from the balloon. Does it move toward the comb, or away from it? Can you make the water defy gravity and move up toward the comb? (Fig. 2)

STEP 6: Repeat step 5 with a balloon inflated with air and charged by rubbing it on your hair. Does the stream of water behave the same way? (Fig. 3)

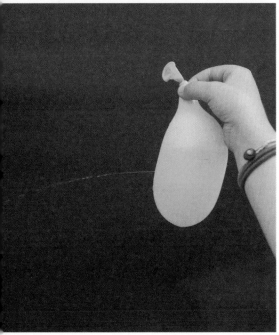

Fig. 1: Hold the balloon so a thin stream of water is coming out the side.

Fig. 3: Will a charged balloon bend the water?

THE SCIENCE
BEHIND THE FUN:

When you rub a comb or balloon on dry hair, electrons jump from your hair to the comb or balloon, giving the plastic or rubber a negative charge. The electron-depleted strands of hair on your head are left positively charged and try to get as far away from each other as possible, making your hair stand up.

Water molecules are made up of two positively charged hydrogen atoms and one negatively charged oxygen atom. Although water doesn't usually carry either a positive or negative charge, when you hold the negatively charged comb next to a very thin stream of water, the hydrogen atoms in the water will all line up in an attempt to get closer to the electrons on the comb. This is called polarization.

Once the stream of water is polarized, the attractive opposite charges are strong enough to move the water toward the comb.

CREATIVE ENRICHMENT

Try this experiment with a stream of water from the faucet. Does the size of the stream affect how well the experiment works? How does the distance of the comb from the stream affect the attraction of the water to the comb?

BODACIOUS BOTANY

WITHOUT PLANTS, WE WOULDN'T BE HERE.

Joseph Priestly was an amateur scientist who started out doing experiments in his kitchen sink and ended up a famous scientist, credited with being the first person to isolate oxygen in 1774. He noticed that in a sealed container, fire burned something away that animals needed to survive (oxygen) and that plants could replace this mysterious element. This research inspired him to become one of the earliest natural philosophers to hypothesize about the science of ecosystems and our dependence on plants for the oxygen we breathe.

Modern science has shown us that plants are wonderful chemical reorganizers. Using the sun's energy and a process called photosynthesis, they can turn water and carbon dioxide into sugar (glucose) and oxygen. Thanks to plants and other autotrophs, such as algae, Earth has an oxygen-containing atmosphere that can sustain life.

With a few beans, plastic bags, food coloring, and a head of cabbage, you can see how plants germinate from seeds, take up water, and put moisture back into the atmosphere.

WINDOW SPROUTS

MATERIALS

→ Paper towel

→ Scissors

→ Small resealable plastic bag

→ Water

→ Uncooked dried beans, peas, or seeds

PLANT A BEAN IN A PLASTIC BAG AND WATCH ROOTS FORM AND LEAVES EMERGE BEFORE YOUR VERY EYES.

SAFETY
TIPS & HINTS

Dried beans are choking hazards for small children.

This experiment will work best with beans that are not too old and haven't been irradiated. You can soak them overnight before doing the experiment to make them sprout more quickly.

For this experiment, choose a window where the beans you plant get plenty of light, but won't be blasted by intense sun all day.

PROTOCOL

STEP 1: Cut a paper towel in half and fold it a few times so it will fit into the plastic ba

STEP 2: Soak the paper towel with water, squeeze out the excess, and put it into the bag. Smooth it so that it's relatively flat. (Fig. 1)

STEP 3: Plant two or three beans or seeds about 1¼ inches (3 cm) from the bottom of the bag, on the same side of the paper towel. Don't worry if they don't stay in place, b if necessary, stuff a little piece of paper towel into the bottom of the bag so the seeds don't sit in water. (Fig. 2)

STEP 4: Seal the bag partway, but leave an opening near the top so the plants can ge some air.

STEP 5: Tape the bag in a window with the beans facing you so you can watch them they grow. (Fig. 3, 4)

Fig. 1: Soak the paper towel in water.

Fig. 2: Plant two or three beans in your bag.

Fig. 3: Hang the bag in a window, with the beans facing in toward you.

Fig. 4: Soon your beans will start to sprout and grow.

THE SCIENCE BEHIND THE FUN:

Seeds, such as dried beans and peas, contain dormant baby plants. Dormant literally means "sleeping." These tiny plants need certain signals to make them "wake up" and emerge from the seed. Germination is the name for the processes the embryonic plant goes through to sprout from the seed and form leaves.

Environmental signals that plants need to germinate include adequate light, air, and water. Temperature can also play a role in germination.

When a plant first sprouts, it gets the nutrients it needs from the seed. In this experiment, you can see the seed shrink as the plant grows. As a plant matures, it will depend on roots and leaves to collect the energy it needs. Once it reaches a certain size and completely uses up the nutrients in the seed, your window sprout will have to be transplanted to nutrient-rich soil to survive.

CREATIVE ENRICHMENT

Record the beans' germination by drawing and measuring them each day. Record your data in a science notebook. What happens if you do the same experiment, but put one bag of beans in a window and another one in a dark closet?

COLLECTING WATER FROM TREES

MATERIALS

→ Nonpoisonous, leafy tree with low branches

→ Large, clear plastic bag, such as an oven bag for turkeys

→ Small pebble

→ Twist tie or string

→ Scissors

→ Clear bottle

ON A HOT SUNNY DAY, SEE HOW MUCH WATER YOU CAN GATHER FROM A "SWEATING" TREE.

SAFETY
TIPS & HINTS

Plastic bags are suffocation hazards. Supervise young children.

Don't drink the water you collect from this experiment.

This project will work best on a hot, sunny day. Don't use your favorite tree, as this experiment may damage a few leaves.

PROTOCOL

STEP 1: On a sunny day, take a plastic bag outside and put it over a leafy branch, enclosing as many leaves as possible. (Fig. 1)

STEP 2: Place a pebble or small rock in one corner of the bag to weigh it down.

STEP 3: Tie the bag securely around the branch with a twist tie or string.

STEP 4: After 24 hours, collect the water produced by tree transpiration. Simply cut the lowest corner off the bag and catch the water in a clear bottle. (Fig. 2, 3)

Fig. 1: Tie a bag over some leaves.

Fig. 2: Collect the water from the bag

Fig. 3: How much water did you collect?

THE SCIENCE
BEHIND THE FUN:

Plants don't sweat like people, but depending on the temperature, humidity and sunlight, they do shed water.

All plants carry water from their roots to small pores called stomata on the underside of their leaves. These pores release water into the air in a process called transpiration. Transpiration helps cool plants, but is also involved in moving important nutrients from root to leaf. Plants transpire the most on hot, dry days and trees that have drunk plenty of water give off the most water. According to the US Geological Survey, a large oak tree can transpire 40,000 gallons (151,416 L) of water a year!

Transpiring cornfields can add huge amounts of water to the air on hot sunny days, possibly contributing to higher dew points in areas near crops. Some scientists speculate that vast expanses of corn may even add enough water to the air to help fuel thunderstorms under the right conditions.

Normally, the water produced by plants evaporates, cooling them, but in this experiment, we trap the water so it condenses in our plastic bag. As you can imagine, it gets very hot in the bag due to the greenhouse effect. That's why this experiment can damage leaves.

CREATIVE ENRICHMENT

Do different kinds of trees produce different amounts of water on the same day? Do evergreens transpire, or cacti? What happens if you use a black bag, or a white one for this experiment, instead of a clear bag?

Try Lab 46, "Greenhouse Effect," or Lab 47, "Dew Point Experiment," to learn more about water in the atmosphere.

LEAF AND VEGGIE CHROMATOGRAPHY

MATERIALS

→ Pencil

→ Jar or glass

→ White coffee filter
(or paper towel)

→ Scissors

→ Dark green leaf, such as
spinach, and a leaf from a
red or orange tree, if it's fall

→ Small coin about 18 mm in
diameter (dimes work well)

→ Grain alcohol or rubbing
alcohol

Fig. 2: With a coin, rub a line of leaf color onto a paper strip.

USE COFFEE FILTER
CHROMATOGRAPHY TO
SEPARATE THE PIGMENTS
IN PLANTS.

PROTOCOL

STEP 1: Balance the pencil on
the lip of the jar or glass.

STEP 2: Cut a few strips of
coffee filter or paper towel abo
1 ¼ inches (3 cm) wide. They
should be long enough to drap
(folded in half) over your penci
so both ends of the paper are
just above the bottom of the ja
or glass.

STEP 3: Remove the paper from the pencil and draw a pencil line about ¾ inch (2 cm)
above and parallel to the bottom of the paper strip on both sides.

STEP 4: Pick some leaves, or find lettuce, spinach, or green onions in the refrigerator.
Wrap a leaf around the coin and press it down against the line on the left side. Roll it
back and forth to rub color onto the line. (Fig. 1, 2)

STEP 5: If you have a second leaf, repeat the process on the other end of your filter
paper. Get as much color as possible onto each spot. Allow to air dry, or dry with a
blow dryer.

STEP 6: Fill the jar with just enough alcohol so that the bottom of the hanging paper
strip will touch it, but the spots of color will not. Hang your paper strip over the pencil
with the bottom of the strips touching the alcohol. Be sure the strip is hanging evenly s
the color will travel straight up. (Fig. 3)

SAFETY
TIPS & HINTS

Young children must be
supervised during this
experiment because rubbing
alcohol is a toxic substance if
ingested!

Coffee filters work better
than do most paper towels.

Fig. 1: Pick some leaves, or find a few leafy greens in your refrigerator.

Fig. 3: Hang the paper over the pencil so the bottom of the strips, below the lines, touch the alcohol.

Fig. 4: Tape the strips into your science notebook.

STEP 7: Watch as the colors travel up the strip and remove the strip from the alcohol before they reach the top. Allow to dry and observe the separated colors. You can tape the strips into your science notebook. (Fig. 4)

THE SCIENCE
BEHIND THE FUN:

Liquid chromatography allows you to separate pigments, the molecules that give plants color, using paper as a solid medium for the molecules to traverse. In this experiment, alcohol is the solvent that pulls different-sized pigments apart and carries them up the paper at different speeds, depending on how big they are.

Green leaves contain a pigment called chlorophyll, which helps plants get energy from sunlight, water and carbon dioxide, using a chemical process called photosynthesis. In the fall, many trees stop making chlorophyll, which is why other colors in the leaves, like red, yellow and orange, become visible.

CREATIVE
ENRICHMENT

Try this experiment with colorful fruits and vegetables, such as carrots, cranberries, and red peppers. Cut the fruits or veggies with a sharp knife and use the cut edge to make a thin line of color on the coffee filter strips.

Do pigments change when you cook food? Repeat this experiment with cooked spinach versus raw spinach.

NATURE WALK BRACELETS

MATERIALS

→ Duct tape

ASSEMBLE A MOSAIC OF NATURAL BEAUTY ON YOUR WRIST.

Familiarize everyone with poison ivy and poison oak before you set out, and remind kids that unidentified berries should never be eaten.

Fig. 3: Turn your bracelet into a piece of art.

PROTOCOL

STEP 1: Tape duct tape around your wrist, sticky side out. (Fig. 1)

STEP 2: Take a walk outside and search for small leaves, acorns, flowers, and other natural artifacts to adorn your bracelet. (Fig. 2, 3)

Fig. 1: Tape duct tape around your wrist, sticky side out.

Fig. 2: Stick the treasures you find on your bracelet.

STEP 3: While you're walking, look for birds, insects and other wildlife. See how many different kinds of trees you can count.

THE SCIENCE
BEHIND THE FUN:

Studies show that kids are spending more and more time in front of electronic screens and less and less time outdoors. Getting out of the house and into nature, whether it's wilderness, parks, or backyards, may be one of the best things for growing minds and bodies.

CREATIVE
ENRICHMENT

Bring a paper bag on your walk to collect leaves that are too big for your bracelet.

Use a nature journal or science notebook to record what you see and hear on your walk.

When you get home, try to identify some of the plants you've found, or birds you spotted.

LAB 42 VEGETABLE VAMPIRES

MATERIALS

→ 2 large cups, plastic containers, or jars, large enough to hold the base of half of your cabbage

→ Warm water

→ Food coloring

→ Head of fresh napa cabbage

→ Sharp knife

→ Fruits and veggies, such as olives and pepper, for decoration

→ Rubber bands or string

→ Toothpicks

SAFETY
TIPS & HINTS

Plan ahead. For the best result, your "vampires" will have to drink for 24 to 48 hours.

An adult should help young children cut the cabbage.

Fig. 5: Watch your cabbage vampires change color as they "drink" from the containers.

MAKE CREEPY CABBAGES DRINK FAKE BLOOD TO SEE CAPILLARY ACTION AT WORK

PROTOCOL

STEP 1: Fill your containers or jars two-thirds of the way to the top with warm (not hot) water. Add two or more drops of blue food coloring to one container and ten or more drops of red food coloring to the other one. (Fig. 1)

STEP 2: With a sharp knife, cut the cabbage in half vertically, from the bottom up, leaving the top 4 inches (10 cm) or so intact, so the two sections are still attached at the crown. If possible, try to cut down the middle of one of the big leaves, so it will turn two different colors when you do the experiment.

STEP 3: Using rubber bands or string, secure the bottom of each side of the cabbage and make a fresh cut at the bottom, about an inch (a few cm) up from the old cut. (Fig. 2)

STEP 4: Put your two cups side by side and submerge half of the base of your cabbage in the red water, and the other half in the blue water. (Fig. 3)

Fig. 1: Add a different color to each container of water.

Fig. 2: Secure the bottom of the cut cabbage with rubber bands.

Fig. 3: Split the bottom of the cabbage into the two containers, with each half submerged in a different color water.

Fig. 4: Put eyes on your vegetable vampires.

STEP 5: Decorate your "vampires" with eyes and spooky eyebrows made from olives and peppers (or whatever you have in the refrigerator). Secure the decorations with toothpicks. (Fig. 4)

STEP 6: Check the cabbages every hour or so to see how much colored water they're drinking. (Fig. 5)

THE SCIENCE
BEHIND THE FUN:

Like vampires, plants prefer a liquid diet. They survive by drawing nutrients dissolved in water up into their stems, stalks, trunks, branches, and leaves.

Capillary action is the main force that allows the movement of water up into plants. In a narrow tube, on a surface that attracts water, the attraction between the surface and water, coupled with the attraction of the water molecules to each other, pulls water up. Plants are composed of huge numbers of tube-shaped cells that take advantage of these physical forces.

In this experiment, you can observe colored water being taken up, via capillary action, into your cabbage.

Imagine how high the water in giant redwoods must travel to reach the leaves at the top. In very tall trees, a process called transpiration helps the water overcome the forces of gravity.

CREATIVE
ENRICHMENT

What happens if you use ice water for this experiment? Does adding sugar or salt affect your results? If you mix several colors together, are they all taken up at the same rate by the cabbage?

Try Lab 39, "Collecting Water from Trees," to learn more about plant transpiration.

SUNNY SCIENCE

UNTIL A FAMOUS SCIENTIST NAMED GALILEO POINTED A TELESCOPE AT THE SUN TO DISCOVER SUNSPOTS, HUMANS SAW THE SUN AS A SYMBOL OF ULTIMATE PERFECTION, A FLAWLESS GOLDEN DISK IN THE HEAVENS. GALILEO WENT ON TO RECORD HOW THE SPOTS CHANGED AND MOVED AND USED HIS DATA TO DESCRIBE THE ROTATION OF THE GIANT STAR.

Sunspots are areas of visibly reduced brightness that appear as dark spots on the sun's surface. They're caused by magnetic activity and are associated with other solar phenomena, such as flares and coronal mass ejections. You may be able to see sunspots with the solar viewer you can build by using the binoculars in Lab 48.

The sun produces an enormous amount of energy in the form of solar radiation, which warms Earth. Without the sun's energy and the greenhouse gases that blanket Earth to hold some of the energy in, there would be no life here. However, there is a delicate balance between absorbed energy and emitted energy, and since the Industrial Revolution, it's been getting more difficult for Earth to cool itself.

This unit explores the sun and the ability of solar energy to warm everything from water to marshmallows.

SUNSET EXPERIMENT

MATERIALS

→ Clear, aquarium-like rectangular container at least 9 ½ inches (24 cm) long

→ Water

→ Small flashlight with a focused beam

→ White paper

→ Milk

USE WATER, MILK, AND A FLASHLIGHT TO SEE WHY SUNSE LOOK RED.

Fig. 4: The beam will appear more yellow and orange after traveling through the milky water.

SAFETY
TIPS & HINTS

Very young children should always be supervised around containers of water.

PROTOCOL

STEP 1: To see how particles scatter light, fill the plastic container with water.

STEP 2: Shine a flashlight beam horizontally through the longest part of the container onto a white piece of paper held several inches (cm) away from the paper on the opposite side. The spot of light on your paper should look white. (Fig. 1)

STEP 3: Add a few drops of milk to the water and shine your light through the water again. Does the color of the light shining on the white paper change? (Fig. 2, 3, 4)

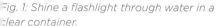
Fig. 1: Shine a flashlight through water in a clear container.

Fig. 2: Add a few drops of milk to the water.

Fig. 3: Shine the light through the cloudy water.

THE SCIENCE
BEHIND THE FUN:

The colors we see depend on the light waves that are reflected and absorbed by the things around us. Light coming to us from the sun contains all the colors of the rainbow. Grass looks green because it absorbs most of the visible light waves except green, reflecting that color back at our eyes. Things that look black absorb all the colored light waves. Blue light has a short wavelength, and easily bounces off surrounding particles in a phenomenon called scattering.

The sky looks blue because air molecules in the atmosphere scatter light waves and only the blue part of the sunlight, traveling over our heads, is scattered enough to reach our eyes. If it weren't for this scattering, the sky would look black, as it does in space. Red light has a longer wavelength and is more difficult to scatter.

Earth's lower atmosphere contains more large particles, such as dust and pollen, which scientists call aerosols. As the sun sets, its light has to travel a longer distance across the atmosphere to reach your eyes and by the time we see it, dust in the atmosphere has scattered out most of the blue light, allowing us to enjoy the red, yellow, and orange light waves that remain to create a beautiful sunset.

Imagine that your flashlight is the sun and the milky water is the lower atmosphere. The molecules in milk filter out the blue light in your flashlight beam, allowing you to create your own red "sunset."

CREATIVE
ENRICHMENT

What happens if you add more milk? Does it make a difference if you use a longer container, so the flashlight beam has to travel farther to reach the paper?

SOLAR STILL SURVIVAL SCIENCE

MATERIALS

→ Large bowl

→ Small bowl, whose rim is lower than the rim of the big bowl

→ 1 cup (235 ml) tap water

→ A few tablespoons (40 g) salt

→ Food coloring

→ Plastic wrap

→ Marble or pebble

HARNESS THE SUN'S ENERGY TO PURIFY WATER.

Fig. 3: Put your solar still in the sun and wait for pure water to drip into the small bowl.

SAFETY
TIPS & HINTS

This experiment works best on a hot, sunny day because it utilizes the sun's energy to clean the water.

STEP 1: Put the small bowl inside the big bowl.

STEP 2: Mix the tap water, salt, and a drop or two of food coloring. This is your "contaminated" water. (Fig. 1)

STEP 3: Pour the salt water into the big bowl, making sure the liquid stays outside of your small bowl, because you'll be collecting clean water in the small bowl.

STEP 4: Loosely cover the top of the large bowl with a single piece of plastic wrap. Place a marble or pebble in the center of the plastic wrap and adjust the wrap so that there is a slight dip directly above the small collection bowl. Seal the plastic wrap around the edges of the bowl as well as you can. (Fig. 2)

STEP 5: Place the bowl in the sunlight and observe it every few hours. Adjust plastic wrap as needed, so condensation drips into the small bowl. (Fig. 3)

Fig. 1: Add salt and food coloring to some water to "contaminate" it.

Fig. 2: Cover the large bowl with plastic wrap.

STEP 6: When you've collected enough purified water, which can take a day or two, you can taste the water to see how your purifier worked. Be sure to wipe the bottom of the collection bowl before you pour it out so you don't contaminate your clean water!

THE SCIENCE
BEHIND THE FUN:

The sun's ultraviolet rays will travel through the plastic wrap and into the colored water, where they're absorbed and rereleased as heat energy. Because the heat can't escape back out through the plastic wrap, the air and water in the bowl heat up.

In your solar still, the warmer temperature helps water molecules on the surface evaporate into the air in the bowl, leaving the salt and food coloring behind in the big bowl. When they collide with the plastic wrap, the water molecules encounter a cooler surface, since the air outside the bowl is not as warm. The clean water then condenses, or forms droplets, on the plastic wrap. When the droplets get big enough, gravity pulls them to the lowest part of the plastic wrap and they drip into the collection container, leaving you with pure water.

CREATIVE ENRICHMENT

Add vinegar to contaminate your water, purify it using a solar still, and check the pH of both your starting and purified water using litmus paper from Lab 29, "Red Cabbage Litmus Paper."

PIZZA BOX SOLAR OVEN

MATERIALS

→ Pizza box

→ Marker or pen

→ Ruler

→ Scissors

→ Aluminum foil

→ Tape

→ Black construction paper

→ Newspaper

→ Clear plastic wrap

→ Dowel or stick to prop the box lid up

→ Snack to warm in your oven (e.g., chocolate, marshmallows, cookies)

SAFETY
TIPS & HINTS

This oven is intended for heating up snacks, such as chocolate and cookies, and should never be used to cook raw meat or anything that can spoil when warm.

Do this experiment on a sunny day.

Very young kids may need assistance cutting the box.

BUILD A SNACK OVEN FROM A PIZZA BOX.

Fig. 3: Your oven is ready to go, with insulation, a window and a reflector. This one needs one more roll of newspaper in the back.

PROTOCOL

STEP 1: Draw a square on the top of your pizza box, leaving a frame of at least 2 inches (5 cm) on each side of the square. Scribble out the line closest to the hinge on the box and cut along the other three lines to make a second hinged lid. (Fig. 1)

STEP 2: Gently fold the flap back along the uncut edge of the square to form a crease. The flap should fold back toward the hinge of the pizza box. Wrap the underside (inside) face of the flap that you made with aluminum foil. Secure the foil with tape outside the lid. This is your reflector.

STEP 3: Open the pizza box and cover the bottom of it with black construction paper.

STEP 4: Stack and tightly roll up several pieces of newspaper. Fit the newspaper rolls around the inside perimeter of the box as insulation. The rolls should be about 2 inches (5 cm) thick. Secure the insulation with tape to the bottom of the box. Be sure you can close the original lid on your pizza box.

STEP 5: Cut two pieces of plastic wrap about 2 inches (5 cm) larger than the hole you cut in the original pizza box top. Open the lid of your pizza box and tape one piece of plastic wrap to the underside of the hole in the pizza box lid. (Fig. 2)

STEP 6: Lift the reflector flap. Tape another piece of plastic wrap over the top of the hole in your pizza box lid. This pocket of plastic wrap is like a double-paned window and creates a layer of air as insulation to keep heat in the box. Make sure the plastic wrap is tight. (Fig. 3)

STEP 7: Take your oven outside, put it on a flat surface facing the sun, and put the food you want to cook inside, on the black paper. Close the lid tightly and open the foil reflecting flap so sunlight strikes the black paper and food in the oven. (Fig. 4)

STEP 8: Prop open the reflecting flap, using a dowel or stick or the ruler. Play with the angle of the flap to see how much sunlight you can get to reflect from the foil lid directly onto the food in the oven.

STEP 9: Wait for your oven to heat up. Check every 5 minutes to see how well your food is being heated by solar thermal energy. When it's done, enjoy your snack. (Fig. 5)

Fig. 1: Cut three sides of a square into the lid of your box to create a hinged lid.

Fig. 2: Tape plastic wrap on both sides of the hole on your pizza box lid.

Fig. 4: Position your oven in the sun, with the foil reflecting light into the box.

Fig. 5: Enjoy your snack.

THE SCIENCE
BEHIND THE FUN:

The sun's rays travel through the double layers of plastic wrap and are absorbed by the black paper at the bottom of your oven, where they're converted to heat energy. This new form of energy can't escape the plastic wrap and the newspaper insulation you added helps keep the heat energy captive in the oven.

The aluminum foil reflector you made directs additional ultraviolet rays into your oven, adding more energy to the mix. As your solar oven sits in the sun, more and more energy enters the pizza box, but most of it can't escape. The increasing heat energy drives up the temperature inside your oven, making it hot enough to warm your snack.

CREATIVE
ENRICHMENT

Use a thermometer to monitor the oven temperature. How warm will your oven get on a sunny day versus on a cloudy day? Does the air temperature outside the oven have an effect on oven temperature?

 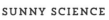

GREENHOUSE EFFECT LAB

MATERIALS

→ 4 identical jars without lids

→ Water

→ Ice cubes

→ Newspaper (black and white)

→ White paper

→ Black paper

→ 3 large resealable plastic bags

→ Thermometer

SEE HOW THE SUN'S ENERGY CAN BE TRAPPED BY PLASTIC.

Fig. 3: Seal all the jars but one in plastic zipp[er] bags.

SAFETY
TIPS & HINTS

This experiment will work best on a sunny day.

PROTOCOL

STEP 1: Fill each jar halfway full of water. Each jar should contain the same amount of water. (Fig. 1)

STEP 2: Outside, in a sunny spot, set two of the jars on pieces of newspaper, one jar on the black paper, and one jar on the white paper.

STEP 3: To each jar, add five ice cubes. (Fig. 2)

STEP 4: Place each of the jars, except one of the jars sitting on newspaper, in a resealable plastic bag and seal it shut. (Fig. 3)

STEP 5: Measure the water temperature in each of the jars after 1 hour. Reseal the jars in the bags, wait another hour and measure the temperature again. (Fig. 4)

THE SCIENCE BEHIND THE FUN:

The clear plastic bags in this experiment are one way tickets for solar energy. Sunlight can enter to warm the air and water, but it turns to heat energy, which can't escape, and the air and water inside the bag heat up.

Certain gases in Earth's atmosphere, such as carbon dioxide and methane, are called greenhouse gases and trap heat the same way as the plastic bags in this experiment. Rays from the sun can easily travel through the atmosphere, but are absorbed by Earth's dark surfaces and turned into heat energy, which can't easily escape back through the gases.

You can imagine that greenhouse gases are like a blanket covering Earth, keeping it warm at night when Earth cools. Unfortunately, if the blanket becomes too thick, our planet may become too warm. With the essential role they play in keeping our planet's temperature stable, it's important to keep an eye on greenhouse gas levels and work to reduce activities that add too much of them to the atmosphere.

Unlike dark surfaces on Earth, snow and ice reflect sunlight and can affect how much of the sun's energy is trapped in the atmosphere as heat and how much is reflected back out into space. This is one reason scientists are interested in studying the polar ice caps. Did you see a temperature difference in the jar sitting on a white surface and the one sitting on a black surface?

Fig. 1: Fill four jars halfway up with water.

Fig. 2: Add five ice cubes to each jar.

Fig. 4: After one hour, measure the temperature of the water in each jar.

CREATIVE ENRICHMENT

What happens if you cover one of the jars with foil? What other variables could you introduce to this experiment?

LAB 47
DEW POINT EXPERIMENT

MATERIALS

→ Empty aluminum can

→ Can opener

→ Warm tap water

→ Thermometer

→ Ice cubes

→ Spoon

MAKE YOUR OWN WEATHER STATION WITH AN ALUMINUM CAN AND A THERMOMETER.

Fig. 3: Watch for condensation to form on the can.

SAFETY
TIPS & HINTS

Aluminum cans are sharp. Young children should be supervised during this experiment.

Depending on the day, you may have to add many ice cubes before you observe condensation on the can. Be patient.

PROTOCOL

STEP 1: Use a can opener to cut the top from the aluminum can.

STEP 2: Fill the can halfway full with warm tap water. (Fig. 1)

STEP 3: Put your thermometer in the water and measure the temperature.

STEP 4: Add one ice cube to the water and stir until it melts. Observe the aluminum on the outside of the can for signs of condensation as you stir. If you see condensation begin to form, immediately check and record the temperature. This is the dew point temperature. (Fig. 2)

Condensation refers to microscopic droplets of water that will give the shiny surface of the can a foggy appearance. You'll notice it first below the water line. Once water starts to condense, you'll be able to draw a stripe in the condensation with your finger. (Fig. 3)

Fig. 1: Fill a can halfway up with warm tap water.

Fig. 2: Add ice cubes, one at a time, to the can, stirring until they melt.

Fig. 4: Record the dew point temperature when you see condensation.

STEP 5: If there's no condensation, add another ice cube and stir until it melts. Continue to monitor the can.

STEP 6: Keep adding ice cubes, one at a time, and stirring until they melt until you see condensation. Record the dew point temperature. (Fig. 4)

STEP 7: Go outside and measure the air temperature. How does it compare to the dew point? Does it feel humid?

THE SCIENCE
BEHIND THE FUN:

The dew point indicates how much moisture is present in the air by telling you the temperature at which water vapor in the air will condense into liquid water as fast as it can evaporate.

When the temperature of the water in the aluminum can drops to the dew point temperature of the air, condensation forms on the shiny metal, telling you that you've reached the point of equilibrium.

On mornings when the air temperature is the same as the dew point, water vapor in the air condenses on solid surfaces, such as grass, forming dew.

CREATIVE
ENRICHMENT

What happens if you repeat this experiment over a number of days? Does the dew point remain constant? How does the relationship between the dew point and the outside temperature affect how humid it feels?

SHOEBOX SOLAR VIEWER

MATERIALS

→ Shoebox with lid removed

→ Piece of white paper

→ Tape

→ Scissors

→ Aluminum foil

→ Straight pin

Fig. 4: Stand with the sun directly behind you.

Fig. 1: Cover one end of a shoebox with white paper.

SAFELY OBSERVE THE SUN USING A SHOEBOX AND SOME PAPER.

PROTOCOL

STEP 1: Cover one interior end of the shoebox with white paper. This is your viewing screen. (Fig. 1)

STEP 2: Cut a large, square notch out of the opposite end of the shoebox and tape aluminum foil over the notch you cut out. (Fig. 2)

STEP 3: Use a pin to poke a hole slightly larger than the pinhead, in the center of the foil. If you make a mistake, replace the foil and try again. The smaller the hole, the sharper the focus will be. (Fig. 3)

STEP 4: Go outside and stand with the sun directly behind you. (Fig. 4)

STEP 5: Hold the box, upside down, with the pinhole pointed at the sun behind you. The foil should be behind your line of sight so it's not reflecting the sun in your eyes. Correct the angle of your box so the sun shines through the pinhole and its image is projected on the white paper as a tiny circle. (Fig. 5)

Fig. 2: Cut a large notch in the end of the box opposite the white paper.

Fig. 3: Poke a pinhole in the center of the foil covering the notch.

Fig. 5: The sun's image will be projected on the white paper as a small white circle.

With a pair of binoculars and a camera tripod, you can make a solar viewer that may make it possible to project the sun's image on a piece of white paper so that it's large enough to see some sunspots. ***Remember not to look at the sun through the binoculars!***

Using duct tape or a clamp, attach the binoculars to your tripod so that the eyepieces are pointing away from the sun and the bigger ends are pointing toward the sun. Hold up a piece of paper and adjust the angle of the binoculars on the tripod until you see double suns (there are two lenses) appear on your paper. Adjust the angle further so just one of the images appears in the middle of the shadow of the binoculars. This will make it easier to see. The further from the binoculars you hold the paper, the bigger the image will appear.

Mount some binoculars on a tripod.

The sun's image will appear as two circles.

THE SCIENCE
BEHIND THE FUN:

When light rays from the sun enter the tiny pinhole, called an aperture, they form an upside-down image of the sun on the paper behind the foil. The image is upside down due to the angle at which the rays of light enter the pinhole and continue on to the paper. This allows you to see the sun without actually looking directly at it.

UNIT
12

ROCKET SCIENCE

WHEN PEOPLE TALK ABOUT ROCKET SCIENCE, THEY'RE USUALLY REFERRING TO AEROSPACE ENGINEERING. WE DEPEND ON ROCKETS TO CARRY EVERYTHING FROM SATELLITES TO TELESCOPES AND ASTRONAUTS TO SPACE. ALTHOUGH THEY'RE JUST MACHINES, ROCKETS HAVE INSPIRED OUR IMAGINATION FAR MORE THAN ANY EARTHBOUND SPORTS CAR.

In 1969, rockets changed our view of what's possible by carrying humans to the moon. From 1981 to 2011, NASA's space shuttle program allowed the construction and maintenance of the International Space Station, which astronauts use to this day to study the universe and our own planet. In 1977, a rocket propelled NASA's Voyager I spacecraft on an unprecedented mission that's carried it beyond the confines of our solar system. Only time will tell what the future holds for space exploration.

While designing a rocket, aerospace engineers have to consider everything from construction materials and the shape of the vehicle to fuel composition. Getting a spacecraft into orbit is complicated, but ultimately comes down to the most basic laws of physics.

Three important physical forces act on all rockets. Thrust is the force lifting the rocket. Drag is the force acting against the rocket, which is caused by air resistance in Earth's atmosphere. Weight is the third important force, and is produced by gravity dragging down the mass of the rocket. With a good background in math and science, engineers can figure out how to maximize a vehicle's propulsion while minimizing its drag and weight.

This unit lets you play with these concepts by making your own, simple rockets and an aerodynamic breath-propelled projectile. At the end, I included an experiment related to electromagnetic radiation, which many scientists involved in research about the universe find very interesting. The project involves microwaves, which travel at the same speed as light.

LAB 49 FILM CANISTER ROCKETS

MATERIALS

→ Film canister with a lid that pops into the end (many shops that develop film will give you discarded canisters, or see the resources section on page 141 for a website where you can buy them)

→ Construction paper

→ Scissors

→ Ruler

→ Paper

→ Tape

→ Drinking glass

→ Pencil

→ Markers and stickers for decoration

→ Chewing gum

→ An effervescent antacid tablet, such as Alka-Seltzer

→ Water

USE A SIMPLE CHEMICAL REACTION TO LAUNCH A HOMEMADE ROCKET.

Fig. 6: Launch your rocket by flipping it over and setting it on a flat surface.

SAFETY TIPS & HINTS

Supervise small children with seltzer tablets because they are medicine.

Some kids may need assistance with popping the lid onto the canister. Have them practice a few times, before you start the experiment.

Wear eye protection, such as safety glasses or sunglasses, when you shoot off the rockets.

PROTOCOL

STEP 1: Cut your paper into a 6 x 4-inch (15 x 10 cm) rectangle, tape it to the film canister the long way, with the paper's edge just above the open end of the canister, wrap it around to make a long tube, and tape it tightly. (Fig. 1)

STEP 2: Trace a drinking glass and cut around the circle you made. Cut out one-quart of the circle and roll the remaining circle into a cone to fit on the end of your rocket. Ta the cone to the end of your rocket, opposite the open end of the film canister. (Fig. 2,

STEP 3: Cut three small triangles from your paper and tape them, evenly spaced, to the bottom of your rocket as fins. Decorate your rocket with markers and stickers. (Fig. 4)

STEP 4: To launch your rocket, put on your safety goggles and chew a piece of gum. you chew, practice popping the lid onto your film canister rocket. When the gum is so remove the lid from the film canister and stick the chewed gum to the inside of the filr canister lid. Break a seltzer tablet in half and firmly stick half the tablet into the gum. S the lid to one side. (Fig. 5)

STEP 5: Turn your rocket upside down and fill the film canister about halfway up with water.

STEP 6: Find a flat surface where your rocket won't tip over. Double check that your seltzer tablet is still firmly stuck in the gum.

STEP 7: Grasping the canister end of your rocket upside down in one hand, and the canister lid in the other, pop the lid with the seltzer tablet on tightly. The tablet should not contact the water.

STEP 8: Flip your rocket over and quickly set it on the flat surface. Stand back and wait for the pressure formed by the chemical reaction between the tablet and water to build up and blow the lid off the canister, launching your rocket into the air. Be patient; it may take 30 seconds to a minute! (Fig. 6)

Fig. 1: Roll paper around a film canister.

Fig. 2: Cut out a nose cone for your rocket.

Fig. 3: Tape the nose cone to your rocket.

Fig. 4: Decorate your rocket.

Fig. 5: Stick half a seltzer tablet in the chewed gum in the film canister lid.

THE SCIENCE
BEHIND THE FUN:

Three important forces act on rockets: thrust (the force lifting the rocket), drag (force acting against the rocket caused by air resistance), and weight (the force produced by gravity dragging down the mass of the rocket).

Pressure builds up inside the canister as carbon dioxide gas is produced by the chemical reaction between water and the seltzer tablet. The gas is rapidly expelled from the film canister when the lid blows off. This thrust pushes the rocket in the opposite direction, demonstrating Newton's third law: For every action, there is an equal and opposite reaction. Drag and weight quickly bring your rocket back down to Earth.

Real rockets have enough fuel to produce plenty of thrust to carry them outside Earth's atmosphere.

CREATIVE ENRICHMENT

What happens if you change the size or shape of the fins? Can you make a parachute to slow your rocket's descent?

EASY STRAW ROCKETS

MATERIALS

→ Printer paper

→ Ruler

→ Scissors

→ Pencil

→ Plastic drinking straw

→ Tape

Young kids may need help taping their rockets.

DESIGN THE ULTIMATE BREATH-PROPELLED PROJECTILE.

Fig. 3: Use your breath to propel your rocket into the air.

PROTOCOL

STEP 1: For the body of your rocket, cut a strip of paper 2 inches (5 cm) wide and 8 ½ inches (21.5 cm) long.

STEP 2: Wrap the rectangle of paper around a pencil the long way and tape it well, so it holds its shape. (Fig. 1)

STEP 3: Remove your rocket from the pencil, fold one end over, and tape it down. This will be the nose of your rocket.

Fig. 1: Roll and tape paper around a pencil.

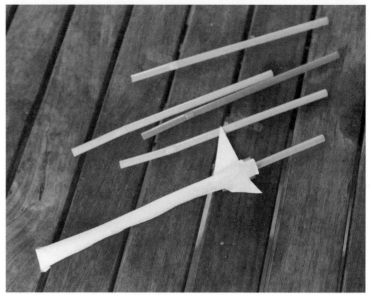

Fig. 2: Make fins for your rocket.

STEP 4: Cut triangles from paper to make fins and tape them on the bottom of your rocket, opposite the nose. Fins work best taped on at right angles, or near right angles. (Fig. 2)

STEP 5: Decorate your rocket with markers.

STEP 6: Put your rocket over the end of a straw and use the force of your breath to launch it. (Fig. 3)

THE SCIENCE
BEHIND THE FUN:

Paper rockets demonstrate how real rockets fly through the atmosphere.

Drag is the force of air getting in the way of your rocket. Weight also drags your rocket down as gravity pulls on it. The lighter you make your rocket (less paper, less tape), and the less drag it has, the farther it will go!

Fins stabilize a rocket's flight. The size and design of the fins affect how well it can be controlled.

CREATIVE
ENRICHMENT

Record your flight lengths. How far does your rocket fly? Try making longer and shorter rockets to see how flight length is affected. What happens if you change the shape or number of fins? How does the angle of your launch affect the flight trajectory?

SKY-HIGH BOTTLE ROCKETS

MATERIALS

→ Cardboard box, such as a shoebox

→ Scissors

→ 1 or 2 liter-size plastic bottles from a carbonated beverage

→ Cork that will fit in the mouth of the plastic bottle

→ Serrated knife

→ Water

→ Needle for inflating balls

→ Bike or ball pump

HAVE A BLAST LEARNING PHYSICS AS YOU LAUNCH BOTTLE ROCKETS, USING WATER AND A BIKE PUMP.

Fig. 5: As air pressure pushes the cork and water out of the bottle, the rocket takes off in the opposite direction.

PROTOCOL

STEP 1: Make a launch pad by cutting the cardboard box so that it will hold the bottle upside down, at about a 45-degree angle. The inflating end of the bike pump must have access to the mouth of the bottle.

STEP 2: Find a cork that will fit your plastic bottle. Have an adult carefully cut the cork in half with a serrated knife. Push the inflation needle through one half of the cork until it pokes out of the opposite side. Use the hole from the corkscrew as a guide, to make it easier. (Fig. 1)

STEP 3: Fill the plastic bottle about two-thirds of the way full of water, attach the needle to the bike pump, and insert the cork in the bottle. (Fig. 2)

Fig. 1: Push an inflation needle through half of a cork.

Fig. 2: Fill the bottle two-thirds of the way with water.

Fig. 3: Set the bottle in the launch pad with the bottom of the bottle pointing up and away from you.

STEP 4: Set the bottle, cork side down, in the cardboard box so that the bottom of the bottle is pointing up, but away from you. (Fig. 3)

STEP 5: Stand behind the launch pad, put your safety goggles on, and prepare for blastoff. (Fig. 4)

STEP 6: Start pumping air into the bottle. The air pressure will build in the bubble at the top of the rocket. When the pressure gets high enough, it will force the cork and water out of the bottom of the bottle with lots of force. As the water shoots down, the rocket will shoot up! (Fig. 5, 6)

Fig. 4: Start pumping air into the bottle.

Fig. 6: Blast off!

THE SCIENCE
BEHIND THE FUN:

Although these rockets lack fins, a payload, and a nose cone, they're very similar to real rockets. Whereas NASA's rockets use rocket fuel as their working mass, these rockets use water. As pressurized air forces the water out of your rocket, the rocket moves in the opposite direction, just as Newton's Third Law says it will: "For every action, there is an equal and opposite reaction."

CREATIVE
ENRICHMENT

What happens if you add more or less water to your rocket?

EDIBLE ELECTROMAGNETIC WAVE EXPERIMENT

MATERIALS

→ Microwave oven

→ Large chocolate bars or sliced cheese

→ Flat microwavable plate

→ Ruler

→ Calculator

SAFETY
TIPS & HINTS

An adult should supervise microwave use.

If using cheese, make sure slices are all the same thickness for better results.

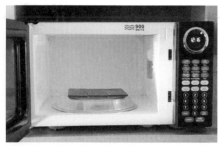

Fig. 1: Set the chocolate bars in a microwave with the rotating device removed.

MEASURE THE APPROXIMATE WAVE SPEED OF MICROWAVE RADIATION, AND EAT THE LEFTOVERS.

PROTOCOL

STEP 1: Remove the rotating device from your microwave. The experiment won't work if the food is moving.

Fig. 4: Calculate the speed of microwaves, based on your measurement.

STEP 2: Flip a flat microwavable plate or dish upside down and set a few chocolate bars or cheese slices side by side on the plate to make a continuous food surface. Think of the food as an artist's canvas that the microwaves will mark. (Fig. 1)

STEP 3: Put the plate in the microwave and cook the chocolate or cheese on high for about 15 seconds. (Fig. 2) Without removing the plate from the microwave, check to see whether there are melted spots. If there are none, cook for another 10 seconds and check again. When you see small melted spots, remove the plate from the microwave.

STEP 4: Use a ruler to measure the distance between melted spots (in cm). These spots are areas where the microwaves hit the food repeatedly in the same place, and represent part of a wave pattern. This number will probably be around 6 cm, or 0.06 meters, but may vary depending on the size of the melted area and the wave frequency (gigahertz) of the microwave oven you're using. (Fig. 3)

STEP 5: To calculate wave length, multiply your measurement by 2, because microwave ovens produce standing waves, which peak at only half the actual wavelength of microwaves. Convert centimeters to meters by moving the decimal point two places to the left.

STEP 6: Once you've calculated a wavelength in meters, you can use that number to calculate the approximate speed of the microwaves in your oven. Multiply the wavelength by the wave frequency of your microwave oven. The frequency of most microwaves is 2,450,000,000 hertz (2.45 gigahertz), but you can double check the label on your oven.

For example, when we did this experiment a number of times, the distance between our spots was usually between 5 and 7 cm. The average, 6 cm, is the same as 0.06 meters. Here is our math: 0.06 m/wave x 2 x 2,450,000,000 waves/s = 294,000,000 m/s. So, we estimated the speed of the electromagnetic microwaves in our oven as traveling around 294,000,000 m/s.

STEP 7: Compare your result to the speed of light (299,792,458 m/s). Is it close? Microwaves and light travel at the same speed, but it's much easier to measure microwaves. (Fig. 4)

STEP 8: Eat your experiment. (Fig. 5)

Fig. 2: Cook chocolate bars on high for about 15 seconds.

Fig. 3: Use a ruler to measure the distance between the melted spots.

Fig. 5: Bon appétit!

THE SCIENCE
BEHIND THE FUN:

Light and microwaves are both forms of electromagnetic radiation (EMR). Other forms of electromagnetic radiation include radio waves, ultraviolet light and X-rays.

You can imagine the way this radiation moves by thinking about ripples on a pond. Electromagnetic radiation moves through space in waves, and each type of EMR has its own wavelength. Microwaves have a much longer wavelength than visible light, and are easier to measure.

All electromagnetic waves travel at the same speed. Because microwaves and light travel at the same speed, if you calculate the speed of a microwave, you should come up with an answer that's close to the speed of light when you do this experiment.

CREATIVE
ENRICHMENT

Repeat the experiment several times to get an average distance between spots and use scientific notation in your calculations. How could you measure the distance more precisely? Would another food or material work better?

Ava	Cooper	John	Cece	Georgia	Croix	Reagan	Jace
May	Henri	Charlie	Claire	AJ	Nicholas	Kate	Bristow
Scarlett	Cela	Lila	Liz	Ava	Natalie	Miriam	Lauren
Sarah	Geneva	Lily	Ella	Hailey	Enzo	Claire	Whitney
Nick	Elena	Nico	Lyuda	Catherine	Stella	Mia	Alessa
Emmett	Nate	Theo	Will	Sienna	Corah	Ayla	Norah
Sarah	Mark	Charlie	Andrew	Carissa	Kyra	Harper	Ian

RESOURCES

CHEMISTRY
acswebcontent.acs.org/scienceforkids/index.html

MICROBIOLOGY
sciencebuddies.org/science-fair-projects/project_ideas/
MicroBio_Interpreting_Plates.shtml

CLIMATE
climate.nasa.gov
climatekids.nasa.gov

ROCKET SCIENCE
jpl.nasa.gov/education/students
nasa.gov/audience/forkids/kidsclub/flash/#.Unj_fvmsi-0

WATER
education.usgs.gov
ga.water.usgs.gov/edu/watercycle-kids-adv.html

KAYE EFFECT
skullsinthestars.com/2013/03/29/physics-demonstrations-
a-short-discussion-of-the-kaye-effect

LIGHT AND COLOR
education.web.cern.ch/education/Chapter2/Intro.html

OCEANS/OCEAN ACIDIFICATION
noaa.gov
pmel.noaa.gov/co2

RENEWABLE ENERGY
nrel.gov/science_technology

CRYSTALS
smithsonianeducation.org/educators/lesson_plans/
minerals/minerals_crystals.html

STATIC ELECTRICITY
loc.gov/rr/scitech/mysteries/static.html

SOLAR SCIENCE
solarscience.msfc.nasa.gov

ALL THINGS SPACE AND EARTH SCIENCE
nasa.gov

FILM CANISTERS
filmcanistersforsale.com

ABOUT THE AUTHOR

Liz Heinecke has loved science since she was old enough to inspect her first butterfly.

After working in molecular biology research for ten years and getting her master's degree, she left the lab to kick off a new chapter in her life as a stay-at-home mom. Soon she found herself sharing her love of science with her three kids as they grew, journaling their science adventures on her KitchenPantryScientist website.

Her desire to spread her enthusiasm for science to others soon led to a regular segment on her local NBC affiliate, an opportunity to serve as an Earth Ambassador for NASA, and the creation of an iPhone app, with the goal of making it simple for parents to do science with kids of all ages, and for kids to experiment safely on their own.

You can find her at home in Minnesota, wrangling her kids, writing for her website, updating the KidScience app, teaching microbiology to nursing students, singing, playing banjo, painting, running, and doing almost anything else to avoid housework.

Liz graduated from Luther College and received her master's degree in bacteriology from the University of Wisconsin, Madison.

ACKNOWLEDGMENTS

Without my family, friends, teachers, and role models, this book wouldn't exist. Thank you especially to the following people, in order of appearance:

My mom, Jean, a culinary genius who showed me how to be fearless in the kitchen, trained me to be resourceful and improvise, and who was always willing to let me make a mess.

My dad, Ron, a brilliant physicist who taught me to love science, patiently assisted me with algebra, constantly encouraged my curiosity, and still answers my questions about physics.

My sister, Karin, who has explored countless backyards, beaches, and mountains by my side, and who experimented with cornstarch at a very young age.

My life-long friend Sheila, who is living her dream of being an engineer and told me how to make a pizza box solar oven.

My best friend Ken, who also happens to be my husband, makes me laugh every day and works much too hard so that I can stay home writing and experimenting.

Richard Smith and Jon Woods, who trusted me with their research and encouraged me to attend seminars and meetings, rekindling my enthusiasm for science.

Charlie, May, and Sarah, my amazing kids, who helped me see the world like a child again and continue to inspire me daily with their ideas, energy, and tenacity.

All the family and friends who keep me sane and offer constant encouragement, especially my writing mentor Jennifer Jeanne Patterson, and Martha Wells, who secured my first writing gig.

NASA, who inspires me with their outreach programs, scientists, astronauts, employees, educators, and online resources.

The ScienceOnline community, including such scientists as Dr. Greg Gbur, who worked out a simple protocol for a fun Kaye effect experiment and let me share it with my readers.

Kim Insley and NBC affiliate KARE11, who give me an opportunity to demonstrate science on a regular basis and make it a priority to include science education as an active part of their programming.

My editors Jonathan Simcosky and Renae Haines, and Quarry books, for helping me share my love of science with a larger audience in a beautiful color format.

My photographer Amber Procaccini, who spent countless hours capturing the chaos and colors of each experiment brilliantly.

Minneapolis artist and stylist Stacey Meyer, who tamed tresses and color-coordinated many of the best photographs in the book.

Zoë, Jennifer, Molly, and Rebecca, who shared their lovely kitchens and backyards with us.

The smart, funny, beautiful kids whose smiles light up the pages of this book, and their parents, for taking the time to bring them to the photo shoots.

ALSO AVAILABLE

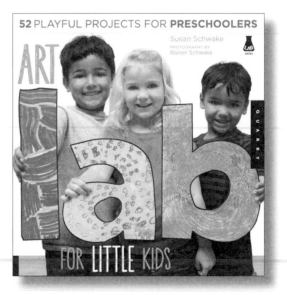

Gardening Lab for Kids
978-1-59253-904-8

Art Lab for Kids
978-1-59253-765-5

Art Lab for Little Kids
978-1-59253-836-2